Oh, Freedom!

Kids Talk About the
Civil Rights Movement with the People
Who Made It Happen

by Casey King and Linda Barrett Osborne

Foreword by Rosa Parks

ILLUSTRATED WITH PHOTOGRAPHS

PORTRAITS BY JOE BROOKS

SCHOLASTIC INC.
New York Toronto London Auckland Sydney

To Sister Francene and Mr. King's class,
to the people who told their stories,
and to all those who gave—and continue to give—their energy, commitment,
and lives to the civil rights movement

ISBN 0-590-67529-X

Introduction copyright © 1997 by Rosa Parks.
Text copyright © 1997 by William C. King and Linda Barrett Osborne.
Portraits copyright © 1997 by Joe Brooks. All rights reserved.
Published by Scholastic Inc., 555 Broadway, New York, NY 10012,
by arrangement with Alfred A. Knopf, Inc. SCHOLASTIC and
associated logos are trademarks and/or registered trademarks of Scholastic Inc.

12 11 10 9 8 7 6 5 4 3 2 1   8 9/9 0 1 2 3/0

Printed in the U.S.A.   23

First Scholastic printing, January 1998

Contents

Foreword
by
Rosa Parks

On December 1, 1955, when I was arrested for refusing to give up my seat to a white man on a Montgomery, Alabama, bus, I became a part of history. I joined thousands of others who worked and sacrificed because they were committed to obtaining freedom. They were ministers, students, teachers, domestic workers, laborers, professionals, and people of all colors who became part of what is known as the modern civil rights movement.

We did not know it was a movement then, with important dates and famous people to remember. We only knew that we were tired of giving in to segregation. We were tired of eating our lunch outside while white people sat at the counter; tired of separate but unequal schools; tired of not being able to vote or to honestly, openly speak our minds. And more than anything, we were tired of living in fear.

How do you capture the feeling of a movement that inspired so many people to action and touched so many lives? How do you then convey that feeling to children?

Most books that talk about the civil rights movement focus on the key events and the important people. *Oh, Freedom!* is different. It is a powerful and intensely personal oral history of ordinary people. And it is unique because the voices of the children themselves can be heard as they respond to their elders' moving descriptions of segregation, protest marches, and tragic assassinations. It is a book that children can relate to because it is the children who ask the questions. The answers help them understand that history isn't just something that happens to other people, but a part of the experience of their families, their neighbors, and ultimately themselves.

I can't think of anything more important to teach young people today than this: that ordinary people working together can change history. They can look for a new Martin Luther King or Rosa Parks or Malcolm X to tell them how to make a difference—but they can also look in the mirror. That is the message of this book.

To live is to have stories. In sharing them, we give a part of ourselves, a part of our lives, to others. That's what makes *Oh, Freedom!* so special. Read it with your children. Answer their questions. Tell them your own stories. And together, stand up against injustice wherever it may occur in the world.

"Been in the Storm So Long"

Life Under Segregation

Today, African Americans sit in Congress and on the Supreme Court, work in medicine, law, and business, and star in movies and television shows. But it was not always this way. At one time, not so long ago, these opportunities were routinely denied to African Americans. As a matter of fact, African Americans were even denied their civil rights—their rights to equality and personal liberty, guaranteed by the U.S. Constitution—and the respect that all people deserve. How did this happen in a country whose Pledge of Allegiance proclaims "liberty and justice for all"?

The answer lies in history. Slavery—the practice of one person owning another—has existed since ancient times. Throughout history, when one nation conquered another, the defeated people were sometimes forced to be slaves. Other people, like the ancestors of African Americans, were stolen from their homes, their land, and their culture, and taken to new countries. In the United States, slaves from Africa were bought and sold like property. Many slave

A handbill from 1784, advertising slaves for sale, which also expressed slave traders' and slave owners' thoughts about Africans in the eighteenth century. They "dehumanized" the slaves— that is, they did not think of newly transported Africans as human beings but as goods to be bought and sold like property. [Note: In the style of printing used in those days, the letter "s" sometimes looked like an "f"—for example, in the words "stout" (first line) and "service" and "just" (third line).]

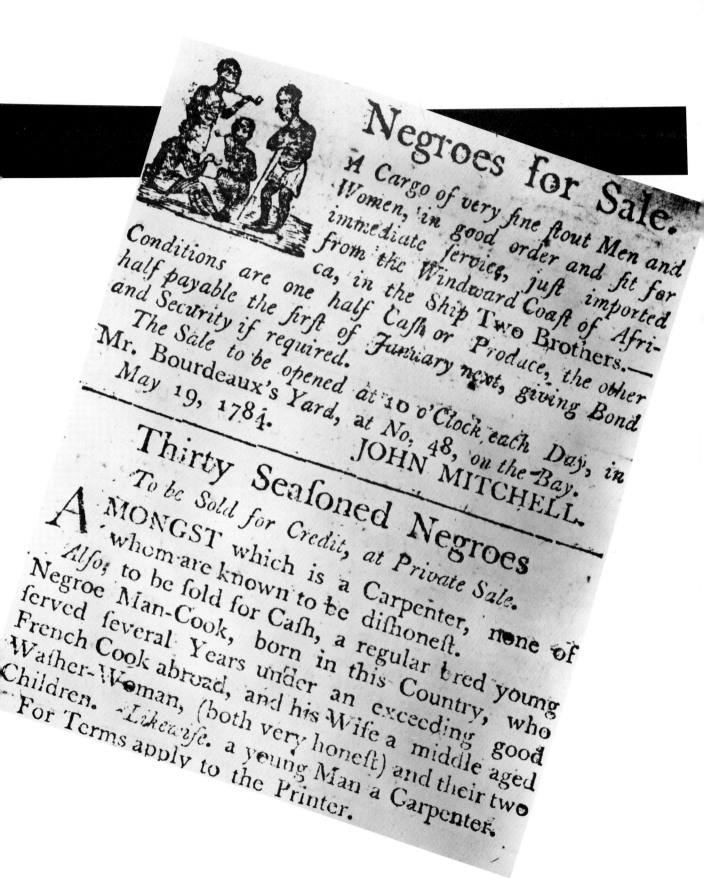

Negroes for Sale.

A Cargo of very fine stout Men and Women, in good order and fit for immediate service, just imported from the Windward Coast of Africa, in the Ship Two Brothers.—Conditions are one half Cash or Produce, the other half payable the first of January next, giving Bond and Security if required. The Sale to be opened at 10 o'Clock each Day, in Mr. Bourdeaux's Yard, at No. 48, on the Bay.

May 19, 1784.   JOHN MITCHELL.

Thirty Seasoned Negroes

To be Sold for Credit, at Private Sale.

AMONGST which is a Carpenter, none of whom are known to be dishonest.

Also, to be sold for Cash, a regular bred young Negroe Man-Cook, born in this Country, who served several Years under an exceeding good French Cook abroad, and his Wife a middle aged Washer-Woman, (both very honest) and their two Children.—Likewise, a young Man a Carpenter.

For Terms apply to the Printer.

owners "dehumanized" their slaves—came to think of them as less than human—and did not treat them as if they were human beings.

Although at first there were slaves in both the northern and southern United States, by the early nineteenth century, slavery had died out in the North. But in the South, most slaves still worked on large farms, called plantations. Plantation owners had invested a lot of money in slaves during the time before machines were able to do the work of many people; the owners quickly came to rely on slaves to do all of the work on their farms. The owners argued that without slavery they would have to pay workers, and would therefore be financially ruined. Their way of life, which benefited wealthy white people, would end.

Frederick Douglass

Many Americans, both black and white, thought that slavery was wrong. Frederick Douglass and Nat Turner were among those who opposed slavery. They were called abolitionists, and they worked to end slavery in the United States.

In 1857, as tensions grew between North and South over slavery, a slave from Missouri named Dred Scott asked the courts for his freedom. Dred Scott's owner had moved and taken him to Illinois and then to the Wisconsin Territory, where slavery was not allowed. Scott felt that because he was now living in a free territory, he should be free. His case eventually reached the Supreme Court, the highest court in the U.S., which declared that a slave was "property" and not a citizen with constitutional rights, whether or not he lived in a free state. The court denied Dred Scott his freedom.

This decision angered many in the North, who continued to pressure the South to end slavery. When Abraham Lincoln was elected president of the United States, the South feared that Lincoln and his Republican Party would finally put a stop to slavery. In 1861, eleven southern states decided that they no longer wished to be united with the northern states. They banded together to form their own country—the Confederate States of America—where slavery would be legal.

Dred Scott

But many in the U.S., including President Lincoln, did not believe that any state should be allowed to leave the federal union. The Civil War was fought from 1861 to 1865 to decide this issue.

During the Civil War, Lincoln issued the Emancipation Proclamation, freeing the slaves in the South. And after the South was defeated, three amendments, or additions, to the Constitution were passed to ensure the rights of African Americans. The Thirteenth Amendment, approved in 1865, abolished slavery everywhere in the United States. The Fourteenth Amendment (1868) promised all citizens equal protection under the law. The Fifteenth Amendment (1870) gave African American men the right to vote.

But people's ideas don't necessarily change just because laws do. Slavery was now illegal, but the feeling remained that black people were "less than human." In the period following the Civil War, known as Reconstruction, black people could own land, vote, and hold office. However, as early as 1865, southern states began passing their own state laws, called Black Codes, which denied black people their rights. Some Black Codes allowed white officials to arrest and fine out-of-work blacks for "vagrancy." They were then sent to work for whites to pay their fines—a situation that recreated slavery. Other Black Codes kept African Americans from owning or renting farms or ruled that they could only work on plantations or as servants.

By the end of the 1800s, the southern states had passed a multitude of new laws that deprived blacks of their rights and kept them apart from white people. This new system of laws was called segregation, a word that means "separation." Segregation severely restricted the political rights of African Americans, their economic opportunities, and their place in society and in everyday life.

The segregation laws were also called Jim Crow laws. The name Jim Crow came from a song performed by Thomas "Daddy" Rice, a white actor. Rice portrayed a black character who was comical, poor, and lazy, and didn't "deserve" the same treatment as white people. Because of Rice's act, people believed ideas about black people that were based not on facts or fairness but on misinformation.

In fact, most white people had little idea of what African Americans were really like, because the Jim Crow laws kept white people and black people far apart from each other in daily life. Black people could not use the same public rest rooms or waiting rooms as white people. They were not allowed to attend "white" schools or sit in "white" seats on buses. Signs hung in public places kept blacks from using "white" facilities. "Colored" was the word used to describe black people; and "Colored Only" and "Whites Only" signs ensured that white Americans would never have a chance to truly know African Americans. They would never have to question their own prejudices—prejudgments about people before knowing anything about them. And the signs also ensured that African Americans would never forget their inferior position.

Black people were also deprived of their legal rights. They were

The cover to sheet music for "Jim Crow Jubilee." Dressed in silly clothes, "Jim Crow" entertained crowds of white people by imitating and insulting blacks.

often tried and convicted of crimes without a lawyer to represent them, even though a lawyer's help is a right guaranteed to every American by the Sixth Amendment. The southern states kept black people from voting by requiring them to take a test that was designed in such a way that no one could possibly pass it. It wasn't just that the questions were hard—some of them had no answers. A famous question of the time was, "How many soap bubbles can you blow from a cake of Ivory soap?" And if black people *did* manage to register, they were often required to pay a fee, called a poll tax, before being allowed to vote.

African Americans could even be arrested for "uppity behavior," the same behavior that was praised as ambition, self-respect, or pride in a white person. Worse still, throughout the South, black people who opposed segregation were often dragged from their houses at night, beaten, and even murdered. The system of segregation was kept in place by fear.

We often think of the civil rights movement—the organized efforts to end segregation and guarantee equality for African

A restaurant in Durham, North Carolina, in 1940. The separate entrances for "white" and "colored" patrons were a common sight in the South during this period.

Americans—as beginning with Martin Luther King, Jr., and the protest marches of the 1960s. But some blacks began challenging segregation as early as the 1800s. When Homer Plessy was arrested in 1892 for riding in the white section of a train in Louisiana, his case went to the Supreme Court. Instead of finding that Louisiana's segregation laws violated the U.S. Constitution, which they did, the Court ruled in 1896 that blacks and whites could be separated in all public accommodations—places like train cars, hotels, restaurants, and even schools—as long as the services offered were equal. This became known as the "separate but equal" doctrine, and it was used to justify and uphold state segregation laws for more than half a century.

Why didn't black people just leave the South? Hundreds of thousands did, moving north to Chicago, Detroit, New York, and other big cities. But many northerners, instead of welcoming them, feared that blacks would take their jobs away. Northern states had few Jim Crow laws, but discrimination—the unfair treatment of people because of prejudices about them— was just as strong against blacks in the North as it was in the South. In the states outside the South, black people were not legally segregated, but they were still denied decent housing, health care, and education. Prejudice and custom kept them from attending white schools or living in white neighborhoods.

May 27, 1942: African American soldiers of Company B drill at Howard University in Washington, D.C. These drills were done in preparation for fighting in World War II, which was taking place at the time.

Following an unwritten law of behavior toward black people, real estate agents did not take them to see homes in white neighborhoods, and most African Americans were forced to live separately in ghettos, which were usually the poorest parts of the city. Black people were prevented from joining labor unions that could help them get better jobs.

During World War II (1939–1945), U.S. troops were segregated, but black soldiers fought and died overseas just as white soldiers did. Black women also contributed to the war effort by working in factories and in other wartime jobs.

When the war ended, black people hoped that, because of their patriotism, courage, and accomplishments, they would finally be accepted as equal in America; but in the South, they found they could still be arrested for drinking from a "white" water fountain, and in the North, they could enter a department store and still not be allowed to try on a hat. It all added up to the same thing: denial of their rights as citizens and denial of the respect they had earned by their efforts in the war. It didn't matter how brave they had been, or how hardworking they were in civilian life. As you will read in the following stories, segregation was still a brutal reality in America, and people continued to suffer from discrimination because of the color of their skin.

Carian Gray with Charles Epps

Carian: My name is Carian, and I will be interviewing Mr. Charles Epps. Where did you grow up, Mr. Epps?

Charles: In a small town: Windsor, North Carolina.

Carian: Was there segregation when you were growing up?

Charles: Yes, there was. The schools were segregated. And the rest rooms at the courthouse were segregated, white and black. If I wanted to use the bathroom, I would have to use the "colored" rest room. And in the movie theaters, we sat upstairs in what they called the crow's nest, while the white kids sat downstairs.

Carian: Is it true that you could not go into restaurants with white people back then?

Charles: That is correct. I remember this little place near the bus station that sold the best hot dogs I ever ate. If you were a white person, you could just go in, sit down, and enjoy your hot dog. But if you were black, you had to go around back. There was a little hole, about twelve inches by twelve inches, and you put your money through that opening. Then they would pass you a hot dog through the hole.

Carian: What was going through your head when you saw segregation happening to you like that?

Charles: You felt something bad when you saw folks inside the restaurant sitting down eating all together in a

Charles: I mean that you are treated as if somehow you were less than human. You weren't treated like a decent person.

Carian: Is it like making a person into an object, like the way they sold slaves?

Charles: Absolutely. And when you're treated like that, you begin to question your worth as a human being. But I always remember what Martin Luther King said—that who you are should be determined not by how you look but by what you stand for.

Carian: I'm sorry you were ever treated that way. This concludes my interview with Mr. Charles Epps.

family, and you had to have the food pushed through a little opening. It was very dehumanizing.

Carian: What do you mean "dehumanizing"?

At this movie theater in the segregated South, black patrons had to use a separate entrance leading to a "crow's nest"—a balcony upstairs.

Brendan Byrne with Jacqueline Wilson

Brendan: Hi. I'm Brendan Byrne, here with . . .

Jacqueline: Mrs. Jacqueline Wilson.

Brendan: So what do you remember about things back in the olden days?

Jacqueline: Back in the olden days—and it wasn't really that long ago—but when I was your age, all the black children went to a different school from the white children.

Brendan: Okay. How were the black schools different from the white schools?

Jacqueline: Well, it was hard to tell because we didn't get to compare.

Brendan: Maybe you just thought it was better. My mom says the grass is always greener on the other side of the fence. She told me that means you always think the things you can't have are better than what you do have.

Jacqueline: That's funny you say that, because their grass really was greener. The white school had beautiful, beautiful green grass on its playground. I lived a half block from that school, and they wouldn't let us play on it even after school. Sometimes we sneaked on with our bicycles because it was just so beautiful.

Brendan: It was right near your house, so why couldn't you play?

Jacqueline: We just couldn't understand why. And of course our mother told us that was the law—that we couldn't go to school with white children, and we couldn't play on their playground, and looking at that playground, you were certainly curious about what other things they had in the white schools that we didn't have in our schools.

The Veasey School in Greene County, Georgia, in November 1941.

Brendan: But there was no way of knowing for sure.

Jacqueline: No, but we had an idea. All of our books had other schools'—white schools'—names in them, and this long list of kids who had used them before us. The materials we got—the sports equipment, the art supplies, things like that—were not as good, almost always used. It made you feel like you weren't good enough to have new things, like you always came second.

Brendan: I'm going to tell my mom your story. The grass *was* greener.

Jacqueline: Yes, it was.

Brendan: All right. This is Brendan Byrne with Mrs. Jacqueline Wilson. That's all.

Dana Little with Loretta Butler

Dana: This is Dana Little, and I'm here with Dr. Loretta Butler. Dr. Butler, did you ever have to sit in the back of the bus?

Loretta: Yes, I had to sit in the back of the bus many, many times in Virginia, and also in New Orleans.

Dana: How come, Dr. Butler, you couldn't just sit anywhere you wanted? I mean, you're a doctor and everything.

Loretta: You see, under segregation, as a black person, you were not protected. Your rights were not protected. In fact, it was just the opposite. The law could be used against you, even if you practiced simple courtesy.

Dana: Like what?

Loretta: Well, one time I was on a bus and I saw a very big, very pregnant black woman standing on the bus. It was very hot and she looked so very tired. So I sat right down in the white section, and then I got up and told her to sit down in the seat I had just taken.

Dana: Dr. Butler, did anyone try to arrest you?

Loretta: No, they didn't do that to

A typical bus scene in the segregated South.

me—maybe because I was really helping the pregnant woman. But the point is that they could have, and that was wrong.

Dana: Thanks for telling me this, Aunt Lo.

Loretta: You're welcome. Give me a hug.

John Ford IV with John Ford III

John: I am interviewing my dad, John Ford. Were you alive during segregation?

John's Dad: Yes, I was. What do you want to know about segregation?

John: What was it like? Was your school segregated?

John's Dad: Yes. Let me tell you something I really remember from that school. It was called the Payne School. It was right across the street from where I lived, so the playground I played on when I was about seven or eight was the playground at that school. And that playground was covered with cinders.

John: What's cinders?

John's Dad: Ashes. See, at one time most homes were heated by coal, and the coal would leave an ash. The people used to have an ash can outside.

John: Like now they have trash cans?

John's Dad: Yes. And they used to have what they'd call an ash man, like a trashman, to come around and get the ashes. And what they did with these ashes was they covered our playground with them—the black kids' playground—because there wasn't grass on it.

January 1953: Parents of children at the Payne School in Washington, D.C., march to demand better facilities from the school board.

John: So the whole thing was covered?

John's Dad: Covered with ashes. And it was rough, too, if you fell down on that stuff, you'd come up with strawberries all over you, you know, scraped skin, and when you got home, your socks were dirty, feet were dirty, full of the coal dust from the cinders on the playground.

John: Thanks, Dad, for talking to me about this stuff.

John's Dad: You're welcome.

Justin Pratt with Marsha Pratt

Justin: Good morning. This is Justin Pratt reporting from North Bethesda, Maryland. I'm interviewing Marsha Pratt. Marsha, what do you remember about segregation?

Marsha: I have many images of segregation from my childhood. Some were in the city and some were in the country.

Justin: I didn't know you lived in the country.

Marsha: Well, I didn't actually live in the country. During the summertime, my grandmother would be at her farm in southern Maryland, and I would spend several weeks with her.

Justin: And that's when you noticed something about segregation?

Marsha: Yes. One Sunday, my grandmother and I went to church together, and we got there very early. My grandmother saw some of her friends outside the church and was visiting with them before we went in. After a while, I decided that I'd just go ahead and find a seat for us in the church and wait for her there. I went in. It was a little country church, and it was so beautiful. I loved the stained-glass windows and looking outside and seeing the cemetery through the windows as the people began filling the church. Then the service began, and I noticed that all the people around me were black people. I was the only person in that part of the church who was white.

Justin: Where was your grandmother?

Marsha: When she came in, she hadn't noticed me, so she was up front in an entirely different section with all the other white people. Then she looked around and saw me.

Justin: Was she mad at you?

Marsha: No. She just sort of smiled and nodded to me, acknowledging that I was fine where I was. But I realized that the black people somehow knew that where we were sitting was where they had to be, and they were not to go where the white people were sitting, up front. And I remember as a child thinking what a funny thing that was.

Justin: Why funny?

Marsha: Well, not funny-funny exactly. Strange-funny, because they had always told us in church that in God's eyes we're all the same. Yet that was where I noticed segregation most vividly, in the place where you'd probably least think you would see it—at church.

Justin: That is funny. Not funny-funny.

Marsha: Strange-funny.

Justin: Okay. Thank you for being with us, Marsha. This is Justin Pratt, signing off.

Alana Brevard with Marsha Brevard

Alana: Live from the Brevard house, my mother here will be answering some questions about living under segregation. What were schools like?

Marsha: Where I went to school in Washington, D.C., my family was the only black family in the neighborhood, and I was the only black child at my school. It was very, very hard because I felt that the teachers didn't like me because of my color. In fact, I had one teacher tell me that Abraham Lincoln was an enemy of the country for freeing the slaves.

Alana: Did the other children like you?

Marsha: The children and I didn't have any problems, but the parents didn't like me. I remember there was a little girl in my classroom named Susie, and she was my best friend. We sat together in school; we did our work together and everything. One day they had an open house, and Susie's mom came to see her. When she saw Susie sitting next to me, she had a fit. She yelled at the teacher, and she pointed her finger at me and said her child was not going to sit next to any "niggers."

Fort Myer, Virginia, shortly after black children began attending schools with white children.

Alana: Oh, my God, Mommy, that's terrible.

Marsha: It was really terrible. And I remember my teacher was upset, not because my feelings were hurt, but because Susie's mother was upset.

After that, they made me sit in a chair all by myself, off in a corner.

Alana: Oh, Mommy, I'm very sorry. This has been Alana, reporting from her house. Thank you.

Nicole Bossard *with* Mary Bossard

Nicole: Grandma, back in the times of segregation, did people feel different or were people against you because of color?

Mary: It depended a lot on where you lived. If you lived in an all-black neighborhood, and you didn't have to go out of the neighborhood for too many things, then you didn't feel different from anyone else.

Nicole: What about when you left the neighborhood?

Mary: Well, that's when you felt different, like a second-class citizen. You felt that you had to be careful where you wanted to go.

Nicole: What do you mean?

Mary: For instance, if you went to a store, you couldn't just walk in and browse around. You usually had a salesperson ignoring you completely—or right on your heels. And if there was a white customer in the store, they would act like they didn't even see you. In many stores, they wouldn't even let you try on a dress or a hat. If you wanted to buy it, they would sell it to you once they were done with the white customers, but you would have to imagine what it looked like on you, or guess if it fit right.

Nicole: That must have made you feel very bad.

Mary: It's a feeling that's hard to put into words. Everywhere you went, you had to ask first: "Can I go in there? Will they accept me?"

Nicole: Thank you for talking to me.

Jessica Nunez and Michael Spurgeon with Malaya Rucker

Jessica: This is our interview with Malaya Rucker. My name is Jessica Nunez and my partner's name is Michael Spurgeon. We are student reporters. Ms. Rucker, what sticks in your head most when you think about growing up during the times of segregation?

Malaya: I'll tell you about the discrimination I remember most, because it probably had the most profound impact on me. I've studied dance all my life, classical piano, classical voice. And when I was growing up, there were very few stars in the ballet or opera who were black.

Jessica: How come?

Malaya: During that time, there were very few opportunities given to people of color who wished to perform classical works.

Jessica: Were there any at all?

Malaya: Yes; Marian Anderson was

Marian Anderson at her outdoor concert at the Lincoln Memorial on April 9, 1939. The federal government arranged for her to sing there after she was barred from singing at Constitution Hall.

one of the women I did see as a role model. In fact, I was named after her. My full name is Marian-Malaya Rucker. Marian Anderson was African American, and she was a very famous singer. She sang all over the world and was internationally acclaimed. But in 1939, when Marian Anderson wanted to sing at Constitution Hall in Washington, D.C., she wasn't allowed to.

Michael: Even though she was famous . . .

Malaya: The Daughters of the American Revolution owned Constitution Hall. They were a group of white women whose ancestors had aided the Revolution. They would not let a black person perform there. Then Marian Anderson tried to sing at Central High School in Washington, which was

Malaya Rucker dancing in the late 1960s while a student at the University of Pittsburgh.

a white school, and the board of education turned her down.

Michael: That's not fair.

Malaya: That's what I've always felt, too. But she was black, and it was during segregation, when talent or achievement didn't always make a difference. There's a good ending to the story, though. The federal government invited her to give an outdoor concert at the Lincoln Memorial, and seventy-five thousand people came to hear her.

Jessica: Okay. Did you ever experience any discrimination like Marian Anderson?

Malaya: Yes, I did in a way. When I was in ballet school, the ballet companies had very few brown-skinned women dancing. I was told that I wasn't the right "type."

Michael: Why? What do you mean, "not the right 'type'"?

Malaya: Our body structures were considered to be improper—our skin too dark, lips too large, hips too big. Even if we were small and thin and met all the other criteria, just our skin color alone would often exclude us.

Michael: Did you do anything about it?

Malaya: I decided that regardless of people's attitudes, I was going to succeed. I've performed in many places throughout the world. I've not allowed experiences of prejudice to stop me, but they still exist, and they probably won't go away for a long, long time.

Jessica and Michael: Thank you. This concludes our interview.

Latoya Smith with Shirley Collins

Latoya: Mrs. Collins, do you remember segregation?

Shirley: Yes, I certainly do.

Latoya: Well, what part of segregation do you remember the most?

Shirley: At one time, the buses were segregated. They had this little piece of wood, and this wood would be placed in some holes on the back of the seat. One side said, "For Colored Only," and the other side said, "For Whites Only," and they would move this back and forth as people got on.

Latoya: Why did they move it back and forth?

Shirley: Well, if some whites came on the bus and there were not enough seats, we were asked to move back, regardless of whether we had enough room to sit down or not. We would get up, and they would move the piece of wood to the next seat down. They would not sit next to us, but they would sit exactly where we had been sitting a few moments before.

Latoya: Why didn't you just share the seat? Sometimes on field trips, they make us sit next to boys.

Shirley: They didn't have to share, and no one was going to make them. They could just make us move. It was the law. We were paying the same price as the others to ride the bus. The whites didn't pay any more, but they were always guaranteed the seats, and we were not.

Latoya: That must have made you feel very bad.

Shirley: Yes, we were very sad and angry about this fact. We knew that this was an injustice.

Latoya: Why didn't you do something about it?

Shirley: Oh, we did. And that is why things are better today.

Latoya: Thank you, Mrs. Collins.

Shirley: You're welcome.

"Woke Up This Morning

"With MY Mind on Freedom"

The Movement to End Legalized Segregation

"Separate but equal." Any African American who spent a day living under segregation knew that "separate" was anything *but* "equal." Charles Houston and Thurgood Marshall, two African American lawyers, set out to prove it. They worked for the National Association for the Advancement of Colored People (NAACP), the oldest civil rights group in the United States. In the 1930s, the two had traveled throughout the South in an old Ford, documenting the tarpaper shacks and drafty log cabins that passed as schools for black children, and the neat, heated brick buildings used for white children.

With the information they gathered, they sued for equal facilities and opportunities in education for black people. In 1940, Houston left the NAACP, but Thurgood Marshall continued to

The Centralia School in Centralia, Mississippi.

argue cases in court on behalf of African American students. Although the NAACP eventually won these cases, it did not challenge segregation itself. The NAACP still worked within the framework of the Plessy decision of 1896: separation of black and white people was acceptable as long as the facilities were considered equal. But by the 1950s, Thurgood Marshall and the NAACP were ready to take their argument one step further: Even if the buildings and playgrounds and textbooks could be made truly equal, segregation was still harmful to black children because the attitude behind segregation dehumanized African Americans just as slavery had done. This was a direct challenge to the Plessy decision.

The case they used to make this challenge involved Linda

Brown, a seven-year-old in Topeka, Kansas. Linda had to attend a black school far from home. To get there, she had to cross dangerous railroad tracks and ride a long way in a run-down school bus, even though there was a school for white children near her home. The Browns filed a lawsuit to allow Linda to attend the white school. The NAACP lawyers combined the Browns' lawsuit with four others to argue before the Supreme Court.

The Court deliberated for a year and a half on this case, which came to be known as *Brown v. Board of Education*. On May 17, 1954, the last day of the Court's spring term, Thurgood Marshall sat in the courtroom as Chief Justice Earl Warren read: "To separate [African American children] from others of similar age solely because of their race generates a feeling of inferiority that may affect their hearts and minds in a way unlikely ever to be undone." The Court ordered schools in all states to be "desegregated," or integrated. The decision was unanimous—all nine justices, including three from the South, had voted to end school segregation.

Brown was a victory for Americans who believed in justice for all citizens. The Brown decision sent a message throughout the South that the Plessy decision—and segregation itself—could be challenged and overturned. It gave new energy to those who were tired of giving in to inequality.

On December 1, 1955, Rosa Parks was sitting on a crowded bus in Montgomery, Alabama. The bus driver noticed a white man without a seat and ordered Mrs. Parks and three other African Americans to stand at the back. The other three did as they were told. Rosa Parks did not. When the driver angrily asked if she was going to move, she answered politely, "No, I'm not." When he threatened to call the police, she calmly replied, "You may do that." That night Rosa Parks, a hardworking seamstress and a member of the NAACP, found herself booked, fingerprinted, and behind bars.

Rosa Parks wasn't the first black person to be arrested in Montgomery for refusing to give up a bus seat. Black leaders had long been thinking about taking action against the bus company, and the time had finally come. They began planning a boycott— an action by a group of people who stop using or buying something in order to produce a change. Black leaders knew that four out of five of the people who rode the buses were black. They realized that if every black person stopped riding, the bus company would lose money.

They decided to hold the boycott on December 5, the day of Rosa Parks's trial. And so, on the day that Mrs. Parks was found guilty of breaking the segregation laws, empty bus after empty bus rolled through the streets of Montgomery.

Rosa Parks is fingerprinted by Deputy Sheriff D. H. Lackey in the Montgomery jail on February 22, 1956, nearly three months after she was fined $10 for violating the city's segregation laws. Mrs. Parks was one of eighty-nine African Americans arrested under a 1921 law prohibiting boycotts.

That night, thousands of African Americans met at the Holt Street Baptist Church to discuss the boycott. The atmosphere was charged with excitement and apprehension. The church filled up quickly, and loudspeakers were set up outside for people who could not get in. A twenty-six-year-old minister took the podium. He had had only a few minutes to prepare his speech, and he was worried that he would not find the right words to say. He stood before the crowd, who watched him in anticipation. Many of

them had never heard his name before: Martin Luther King, Jr.

"We are tired . . . of being segregated and humiliated," King told them. " . . . For many years, we have shown amazing patience . . . But we come here tonight to be saved from that patience that makes us patient with anything less than freedom and justice."

King was a strong believer in nonviolent protest, the kind Mahatma Gandhi, the Indian leader, had used to win his coun-

During the bus boycott, Martin Luther King, Jr., spoke at mass meetings like this one at a Montgomery church, encouraging protesters to keep up the fight.

try's independence from Britain in 1947. He was also inspired by the traditions of the black church, which had retained its independence from white control and promoted the ideals of freedom and justice. King urged the people that night to continue the boycott. He believed that fighting segregation was the right thing to do, and he felt that a peaceful boycott was the right way to achieve it.

For more than a year, nearly every black person in

Montgomery walked, carpooled, or rode in church vans. The bus company lost money, and business fell off in downtown Montgomery. But the bus company refused to give in. It took a 1956 ruling by the Supreme Court to finally end segregated seating on buses throughout the country.

This success prompted Martin Luther King, Jr., and other ministers from churches throughout the South who had supported the boycott to form an organization called the Southern Christian Leadership Conference (SCLC) in 1957. Together they would carry on the protests that began in Montgomery.

Meanwhile, despite the decision in *Brown v. Board of*

Education, the southern states were determined not to desegregate their schools. They passed more than 450 new laws to stop or slow down integration.

In 1957, Arkansas governor Orval Faubus, directly defying the *Brown* decision, called in the Arkansas National Guard to prevent nine black students from entering all-white Central High School in Little Rock. Day after day, white mobs gathered in front of the school, but Faubus refused to take measures to stop the white violence that was taking place. Finally, President Dwight D. Eisenhower was forced to send in federal soldiers to protect the black students and escort them to classes. The next

October 3, 1957: Armed federal troops escort the black students known as the Little Rock Nine as they leave Central High School in Little Rock, Arkansas. (Only seven of the students can be seen in this photo.)

year, Faubus decided to close all the schools instead of integrating them. They remained closed until a Supreme Court ruling forced them to reopen in 1959.

Although the southern states kept resisting, the struggle for civil rights continued to gather strength and to find new expression. On February 1, 1960, four students from a black college sat down at the Woolworth's lunch counter in Greensboro, North

Carolina. They thought they might be beaten or arrested, but the waitress just looked at the well-dressed students, not sure what to do. It was the first time she had ever seen "colored" people sit in the "whites only" section. She did not take their order. The students sat quietly until the restaurant closed; then they left.

Two days later, more than eighty students were "sitting in" at the Greensboro Woolworth's, and within weeks there were lunch counter sit-ins across the South. The response to the protesters varied. Sometimes hostile white people simply watched them or hurled insults. Other protesters were threatened with violence. Food was dumped over their heads; some were beaten, others arrested. John Lewis and James Bevel, two of the student leaders, nearly died in Nashville when the lunch counter manager turned on a fumigating machine. But as one group of protesters left, another would always be there to replace them.

Martin Luther King, Jr., and Ella Baker, Executive Director of the SCLC, were inspired by the young people's courage and determination. Baker helped them form the Student Nonviolent Coordinating Committee (SNCC, pronounced "snick") to lead and organize more student protests.

Sit-ins soon led to "wade-ins" at all-white swimming pools, "kneel-ins" at all-white churches, and demonstrations in front of movie theaters and department stores that discriminated against blacks. Protesters marched peacefully back and forth, fortifying themselves with songs such as "Woke Up This Morning with My Mind on Freedom" or finding unity and courage in sharing verse after verse of "We Shall Overcome" or bravely chanting, "Freedom Now!"

Nonviolent protest was a difficult test of patience and

endurance. Even as white crowds grew increasingly violent, protesters managed to remain peaceful and courteous, sustained by the spirit of love and brotherhood and a deep belief in the effectiveness of the nonviolent strategy, in which they were well trained. Many black leaders also lived with threat after threat on their lives. The Ku Klux Klan, an organization of white people who used violence to terrorize blacks, burned crosses in front of the homes of people who protested segregation. They bombed churches and ambushed, beat, or murdered those who opposed their racist ideas.

Not all white people opposed the end of segregation, however. Over the course of the civil rights movement, many participated in demonstrations, and some risked being threatened, beaten, or killed, just as black people did.

Both black and white protesters took part in the "Freedom Rides" of 1961, organized by a civil rights group called the Congress of Racial Equality (CORE), founded by James Farmer. CORE planned the Freedom Rides in order to test whether states were obeying a federal order that forbade segregation of buses, bus stations, and restaurants that served passengers traveling through more than one state.

On May 4, 1961, seven black and six white Freedom Riders left Washington, D.C., on two buses. Their plan was to ride to New Orleans, using the bus facilities along the way. The two groups never made it. In Birmingham, Alabama, police stood by while a white mob beat the Freedom Riders on one bus. In Anniston, Alabama, the other group of riders ran for their lives when their bus was fire-bombed. Even more astonishing than these acts of violence was the fact that it was the Freedom Riders, not the white mobs, who were jailed for "breaking the peace." Nevertheless, the Freedom Riders refused to yield. Hundreds more poured into the South, and finally, in the fall of 1961, the federal government upheld the rule against segregation in interstate buses and terminals.

In April 1963, demonstrators returned to Birmingham for protests led by Martin Luther King, Jr. By this time, King had

May 14, 1961: Flames engulf one of the first two Freedom Ride buses, attacked and burned outside Anniston, Alabama.

become a prominent leader in the civil rights movement. The movement decided to target Birmingham because it was one of the most segregated cities in the South. City officials had even forbidden the sale of a children's book that had pictures of black and white rabbits.

The police were quick to arrest the demonstrators for trespassing, and later for violating a court order against picketing. Even King himself was arrested. But for each group of protesters taken away, there were new ones, including thousands of young children, to replace them. Police used dogs that viciously attacked

protesters, and firefighters unleashed powerful water hoses, which tore their clothes off and sent them tumbling down the street.

Scenes such as these appeared each night on television news. Across the nation, millions of horrified Americans watched what was happening. People around the country saw for themselves the ugliness and violence underlying segregation and the quiet decency of the protesters.

As newspaper and television coverage increased, support for civil rights began to grow among white people as well as black people. In the wake of Birmingham, President John F. Kennedy introduced a strong civil rights bill in Congress that would end segregation in all public places. But opposition from southern Congressmen had always kept laws like this from being passed. This time black leaders weren't going to take any chances. It was time to bring the message *"Freedom now!"* right to Congress's front yard.

These leaders (including Martin Luther King, Jr.; James Farmer; Roy Wilkins of the NAACP; A. Philip Randolph, who had founded a pioneering labor union for black train porters; and SNCC head John Lewis) planned a march on Washington, D.C., for August 28, 1963. Most of these leaders thought the march should focus on the need to pass the civil rights bill. However, John Lewis and other SNCC members felt they should use the opportunity to forcefully criticize the government for doing so little to end segregation. The more cautious leaders, concerned that Lewis's criticism would undermine the main purpose of the march, convinced him to modify his speech. This experience confirmed the differences in approach between the students and some of the older black leaders.

On the day of the march, however, more than 250,000 people streamed into Washington from all over the country—some on buses, some in cars, some on trains, and some walking. Although it was a steamy summer day, with temperatures in the nineties, the women wore dresses and hats and the men wore

August 28, 1963: Crowds of demonstrators head for their buses home after the triumphant March on Washington. The Capitol is in the background.

shirts and ties. Carrying signs demanding "Jobs and Freedom," they walked together in orderly, organized groups toward the Lincoln Memorial. There they heard the rumbling, powerful voice of Martin Luther King, Jr., proclaim:

"I say to you today, my friends, so even though we face the difficulties of today and tomorrow, I still have a dream. It is a dream deeply rooted in the American dream. I have a dream that one day this nation will rise up and live out the true meaning of its creed, 'We hold these truths to be self-evident, that all men are created equal.' I have a dream that one day on the red hills of Georgia, sons of former slaves and the sons of former slave owners will be able to sit down together at the table of brotherhood . . ."

The 1963 March on Washington was one of the largest demonstrations in the history of the United States. It lasted only one day, but it riveted the nation's attention on the fight for racial equality.

In 1964, Lyndon B. Johnson, who had become president when Kennedy was assassinated, signed the Civil Rights Act into law. The law called for the continuing integration of schools and transportation, and for the desegregation of all housing and public facilities.

Although the 1964 law also reaffirmed the right to vote, southern states continued using poll taxes and other tactics to keep blacks away from the voting booth. In response, SNCC organized "Freedom Summer" in 1964 to educate and register black voters in Mississippi—and to give them something they had never had before: a political party that represented African Americans. SNCC formed the Mississippi Freedom Democratic Party (MFDP) to challenge the state's Democratic Party, which was all-white.

They recruited students from all over the country for this project, including CORE members James Chaney, Andrew Goodman, and Michael Schwerner. In June, when the work had barely begun, these three men disappeared. Their bodies were not found until August. The three had been murdered.

Ruleville, Mississippi: SNCC members Martha Prescod, Mike Miller, and Bob Moses taking part in voter registration work.

Despite the fear their disappearance had caused, the MFDP had 80,000 black members by August. Just days after the bodies of Chaney, Goodman, and Schwerner were discovered, delegates from the party arrived at the Democratic National Convention in Atlantic City, New Jersey, to nominate a candidate for president. Their aim was to get "seated" as official delegates. If they succeeded, they would replace the all-white Mississippi Democrats, who excluded blacks from membership. They would then represent Mississippi.

After much controversy, the MFDP was offered the compromise of two seats instead of the sixty-eight they wanted. They refused, accepting no compromise with what they felt was justice long overdue. Leaders Bob Moses and Fannie Lou Hamer made impassioned speeches, which appeared on television, about the hardships they had endured. They were asked to leave the convention. The experience of the Freedom Democratic Party led some civil rights leaders to doubt whether the government was really willing to give them more than tokens of equality.

Nevertheless, the struggle for voting rights continued in January 1965, when Martin Luther King, Jr., and other African American leaders targeted Selma, Alabama, for their next big campaign. In Selma, only one in every hundred eligible black voters was registered. Demonstrators began by marching to the courthouse several times, and then decided to take their demands to the state capital in Montgomery.

On March 7, as six hundred marchers tried to cross the Edmund Pettus Bridge on their way from Selma to Montgomery, helmeted troopers on horseback clubbed them with heavy nightsticks. Tear gas filled their lungs. The marchers were forced to retreat. But on March 21, they returned—this time guarded by federal troops. White people along the route shot at them, but they made the four-day, fifty-four-mile walk from Selma. Nearly thirty thousand blacks and whites joined the marchers for the final three-mile stretch into Montgomery.

The Selma campaign succeeded in focusing national attention on the issue of voting rights in the South. Congress passed the Voting Rights Act in 1965, ensuring that the federal government would send federal marshals, if necessary, to protect African Americans from harassment, poll taxes, or anything else that prevented their right to vote.

The Voting Rights Act made a difference in just one year. In 1963, fewer than 25 percent of blacks living in Selma and surrounding Dallas County had been registered to vote. By 1966 the figure had jumped to 60 percent. Not only were they able to vote, but soon many African Americans would be elected to county, state, and federal office.

This victory following Selma marked the final chapter in the battle against segregation laws in the South. One hundred years after the close of the Civil War, which ended slavery, legal segregation had finally ended.

Ashley Glover with Helen Wright

Ashley: My name is Ashley Glover, and I am with Mrs. Helen Wright. Her husband was a judge who decided that segregation was wrong and said so, and my parents know her. So here I am. Mrs. Wright, my first question is, What exactly did your husband do?

Helen: My husband, Skelly, was a federal judge in New Orleans when the famous Supreme Court decision *Brown v. Board of Education* called for all schools to be integrated so that black children would have the same opportunity for a good education as white children. In Louisiana, as in many southern states, schools were segregated. Skelly ordered New Orleans to desegregate its schools.

Ashley: That's a good thing.

Helen: Well, not everyone in New Orleans thought so. It was a very hectic, unpleasant time. White women stood in front of schools with their hair curlers on and screamed at and taunted the black children. They had to bring out fire hoses to quell the mobs of people. At one point, they almost shoved Judge Wright into the street to be hit by a car.

Ashley: On purpose?

Helen: One would have to assume so.

Judge Wright received many death threats. The hate mail was incredible. It was an awesome armload of manila folders, probably three feet high, which I took to the department of psychiatry at Tulane, a university in New Orleans, for research.

Ashley: Did the Ku Klux Klan send it?

Helen: Well, most of it was anonymous; there was no signature or address. And I remember I always used to think, if you didn't have the courage to sign your name, you had no business writing.

Poolesville, Maryland: White women and young people display signs protesting the school desegregation taking place in Poolesville schools. The woman on the far right carries a sign that says, "We like you. But we don't want you in our school."

Ashley: Didn't your friends think you were doing a good thing?

Helen: Well, it's interesting, honey. I had a friend who I knew didn't approve of integration one bit. One day, she turned to me and said, "Helen, there's something I just must say to you." And I said, "Oh, now, never mind, we can be friends in spite of the difference of opinion." And she said, "No, there's something I have to say. There are times when I am ashamed to be seen with you." And I said, "Well, I'll tell you something. You need never be ashamed again." And that was the end of our alleged friendship. But there were also wonderful friends who supported us, not just because they felt Skelly was doing what was right, but because they admired his courage. It was a wonderful lesson, if lessons like that are wonderful, in learning who your real friends are.

Ashley: I think that about wraps it up. Skelly Wright died several years ago, but there's a quote on the mantel in Mrs. Wright's home where he talks about how you have to do the right thing no matter how hard it is. He says ending segregation "will require the utmost patience, understanding, generosity, and forbearance from all of us." Thanks, Mrs. Wright, for talking to me.

Matthew Jackson with Ruth Jackson

Ruth: Okay, here are Matthew and Mom, sitting by the side of the bed, going to talk about equal rights . . .

Matthew: Otherwise known as the civil rights movement. And how my mother was involved. Did you take part in any marches or protests?

Ruth: Yes, I did. When I was young, one of the civil rights groups in Kansas City decided that we were going to have some demonstrations, some sit-ins and stand-ins, and we were going to protest at some of the movie theaters where the first-run movies played, where you had the big screens, and the big stereo sound, and safe parking lots, and where black people were not allowed.

Matthew: What grade were you in then?

Ruth: A little older than you. I was in the eighth grade.

Matthew: And you were out protesting?

Ruth: Yes, and it was a tremendous responsibility for seventh-, eighth-, and ninth-grade kids.

Matthew: Did they just throw you out there?

Ruth: No, we had to learn how to protest. We went down on Saturdays to the YWCA, and we did training to be protesters. It was funny. We'd get all dressed up in little skirts and sweaters because they made a big deal out of what you wore. We had to look nice. We'd get into separate lines in the gymnasium of the Y. And one group would be the white people, and we'd be ourselves, and we'd practice marching back and forth, holding up our signs, and just being quiet. And they would practice trying to get us upset. They'd come up to try to push you into what was supposed to be the wall, try to trip you. They'd yell, "Hey, nigger! Hey, coon!"—all the bad things they expected the white people were going to call us—and they would try to snatch the signs out of our hands. And they even spat on us.

Matthew: Wasn't spitting on each other demeaning, even in practice?

Ruth: Sure, but we knew that it was probably going to happen, and we wanted to be ready. We were practicing self-control. Because the idea was that we

Ruth Jackson (third row, third from left) and other members of her church youth delegation in 1957. Several of these young people also trained at the YWCA that summer to picket segregated movie theaters.

were just going to be quiet, we were going to stand there and take it no matter what. And if you weren't able to, if you didn't pass the practice, then you couldn't go.

Matthew: That does sound hard.

Ruth: It was really scary, Matthew, and even when I think about it now, I choke up inside. And some of us didn't make it. Some of the girls would cry; the boys would want to fight back. And if you showed emotion, you couldn't go. Because we didn't want to incite any kind of conflict. We were trying to say, "We're good enough," as if to be good enough to go into a white theater meant we had to have better manners and better self-control than white people who'd be calling us names and spitting on us.

Matthew: Did anybody ever hurt you?

Ruth: Nobody hurt me. Physical hurt wasn't part of it. It was all psychological. I had always learned in history class about America being the great melting pot. I wondered why I had to be defined by my black heritage alone. I guess it's the way we look that makes the difference. People only see us from the outside. I hope that's not always the way it is for you, baby. I hope they see all of who Matthew is. Are you getting tired? I'm getting tired. It's hard to talk about some of these things.

Matthew: All right. Thanks, Mom.

Kaji Spellman with Karen Spellman

Kaji: Hi. This is Kaji Spellman, and I'm interviewing my mother, Karen Spellman. Mom, what kinds of things did you do as a young person in the civil rights movement?

Karen: I joined the NAACP Youth Council when I lived in Greensboro, North Carolina. Your grandfather Dr. Edwin R. Edmonds was the president of the Greensboro NAACP, and I'd go with him to "mass meetings," which were usually held on Sunday evenings at large black churches in Greensboro, Charlotte, or Raleigh. The churches would be filled with hundreds of people. We'd begin with a prayer and a hymn: "Lift Ev'ry Voice." You could hear some of the best music and most inspiring speeches. The meetings were always a real social event for people in the movement.

Kaji: So you enjoyed going?

Karen: Yes, but it was more than that. The mass meetings were our way of keeping our spirits up when times got rough. They also kept everyone informed about the latest civil rights developments. Besides my father, my favorite speaker was Roy Wilkins, who was the national field secretary of the NAACP at that time. He was so cool, speaking in his calm, scholarly manner. He never seemed afraid, just real agitated about segregation.

Kaji: Did you ever meet any other

famous civil rights leaders?

Karen: My favorite was Ruby Doris Robinson, SNCC's legendary executive secretary.

Kaji: Why was she your favorite?

Karen: Ruby was an amazing leader. She was a bold-talkin' sister, even though she was petite and pretty. She was always the first to do the dangerous sit-ins, and she was so well respected by both men and women.

Kaji: What about the Ku Klux Klan? Did you ever meet any of them?

Karen: Well, you don't exactly meet members of the Klan, but believe me, we knew each other well. The Klan, cowards that they were, were always sneaking around in the darkness of night doing terrible things to black people. But lucky for us, they weren't too smart. One time they burned a cross on our front yard—but they didn't know we had moved from the house several months earlier. The only thing they

Members of the Ku Klux Klan wearing traditional hoods and robes to disguise themselves—and their horses—burn a cross. The KKK was formed in 1865 by a group of Confederate Army veterans to keep black people from voting or exercising other rights they had gained after the Civil War. Nearly one hundred years later, they still used cross-burning to scare those who protested segregation.

Karen Spellman (second from left) demonstrates with other SNCC members from Howard University in 1966.

scared was the stray cat that lived under the house. But they still kept calling my father to say they had planted bombs under our beds, which was pretty upsetting.

Kaji: Did you ever have any frightening experiences with SNCC?

Karen: In 1966 SNCC set up the Lowndes County Freedom Organization in Alabama that ran a slate of black candidates for local office for the first time ever. During the day we worked all over the county, but we slept at SNCC's "freedom house," a tiny clapboard house on a lonely country road. At night Klansmen would drive by and shoot into the house. And they would wait by the side of the road behind bushes to ambush civil rights workers. If our lookout spotted a car with its lights off, the driver would push the gas pedal to the floor and zoom by the Klan car. SNCC people were well known for being extremely fast drivers.

Kaji: I'm glad, Mom. Thanks for talking to me about the civil rights movement.

Ruth Welter with Bernice Johnson Reagon

Ruth: Hi, I'm Ruth Welter, here with Bernice Reagon to talk about singing songs and the civil rights movement. Can you remember a time back then when singing gave you a special feeling inside?

Bernice: Yes. After they let us out of jail.

Ruth: You were in jail? What did you do?

Bernice: I was arrested marching for justice in Albany, Georgia. After they let us out of jail, I went to a mass meeting for people who were involved in marching and protesting. That particular night a girl who was in school with me—so she was also a teenager—stood up and spoke about being put in jail and refusing to pay her bail.

Ruth: What's bail?

Bernice: That's when you pay an amount of money the judge orders so you can be out of jail until they have your trial.

Ruth: Why wouldn't she pay her bail?

Bernice: Because she wanted to stay in jail longer to make the point that segregation was really wrong. After she finished talking, I started to lead a song, and my voice was bigger than I had ever

January 22, 1964: Demonstrators at the Forrest County Courthouse in Hattiesburg, Mississippi, sing to show their spirit during "Freedom Day."

heard it before. It was like my whole body was heated up inside from the sound of my voice.

Ruth: How come?

Bernice: I think it was because my voice had blended with the rest of me as a fighter for freedom.

Ruth: There was a lot of singing during the demonstrations, right?

Bernice: Yes.

Ruth: Why did people sing during the demonstrations?

Bernice: We sang because we were scared.

Ruth: Really? When I look at pictures, the marchers don't look scared. They look very brave.

Bernice: Yes, when you look at the pictures it looks like we were really together, and we really knew what we were doing, and we were strong and fierce. But we were scared to death because we'd been told all our lives, "Stay in your place," and we were trying to change that. And I remember marching down the street with my best friend, and then all these police start coming, and you can hear your mama telling you, "Behave yourself," and "Don't ever run into no police." So what do you do then?

Ruth: Go home and hide under the blankets?

Bernice: No, no. You can't do that. So you sing.

Ruth: You sing?

Bernice: You just sing, "Oh, freedom, oh . . ." And sometimes your voice would be quivering at first, but if somebody else joins in, then your voice smoothes out. And then it keeps you marching, and you can sing right over your fear.

Ruth: Could you teach me a song from the civil rights movement?

Bernice: Do you sing?

Ruth: Not really.

Bernice: A little?

Ruth: A little.

Bernice: Will you sing with me?

Ruth: If we can turn off the tape recorder.

Bernice: All right, you can cut it off.

Ruth: Thank you.

The song "Oh, Freedom!" was born during the Civil War, when black soldiers fought for their people, their freedom, and their country.

Oh, freedom! Oh, freedom!
Oh, freedom over me;
And before I'll be a slave,
I'll lie buried in my grave,
And go home to my Lord, and be free.

No more moaning, no more moaning,
No more moaning over me;
And before I'll be a slave,
I'll lie buried in my grave,
And go home to my Lord, and be free.

No more mourning, no more mourning,
No more mourning over me;
(Chorus)

No more weeping, no more weeping,
No more weeping over me;
(Chorus)

No more sighing, no more sighing,
No more sighing over me;
(Chorus)

Oh, what singing, oh, what singing,
Oh, what singing over me;
(Chorus)

Bernard Keith Jarvis with James Farmer

Bernard: This is Bernard Jarvis interviewing James Farmer. Mr. Farmer, when did you first decide to do something about civil rights?

James: I grew up in the South, and it was in Mississippi, when I was three and a half years old, that I became acquainted with segregation. I discovered this in a town called Holly Springs. I could not buy a Coca-Cola in a drugstore downtown even though a little white boy could. I could not buy a Coca-Cola there because of my skin color. And this hurt me badly. I went home, holding my mother's fingers as we walked. When we got home, she cried, and I sat on the porch steps thinking, "Someday my children will be able to buy a Coca-Cola in Holly Springs, Mississippi. I'll do something about it."

Bernard: Is that why you organized the Freedom Rides?

James: Well, in 1961, at CORE, we knew that to get the support of the country behind us to end segregation, we had to have some kind of dramatic project to attract the attention of the press, radio, and especially television. Your generation has grown up with television, but it was not common in this country until the mid-1950s. But it was television, you see, that brought our message to people all over the United States and, indeed, the world.

Bernard: Can you explain about the Freedom Rides?

James: The plan was to have interracial groups riding Greyhound and Trailways buses, with the blacks in front and the whites in back, both refusing to move. At every bus terminal, the whites would go into the waiting room marked for "coloreds" and the blacks into the "white" waiting room. They would behave nonviolently no matter what

happened to them. We started in Washington, D.C., on May 4, 1961, and we hoped to arrive in New Orleans on May 17, the anniversary of the *Brown* decision. Well, we didn't reach New Orleans then. A bus was burned to the ground in Anniston, Alabama.

Bernard: So it wasn't a nonviolent protest.

James: The Freedom Riders remained nonviolent, but they were beaten by angry white mobs. One sixty-two-year-old Freedom Rider named Walter Bergman was so badly beaten that he had a stroke, and he's been in a wheelchair for thirty-three years. Another, Jim Peck, was left unconscious, lying in a pool of his own blood in the alley outside the

James Farmer (second from left) studies one of the Freedom Ride routes with fellow riders, who came from as far away as Arizona to take part.

bus terminal. He had to get more than fifty stitches in his head.

Bernard: Didn't that stop you?

James: No. Students from SNCC in Nashville, Tennessee, joined the Freedom Ride, and CORE students came up from New Orleans. I rode with them, and we were arrested in Jackson, Mississippi. I made the decision we would fill up the jails. If Mississippi had jail cells, we had the bodies to fill them. We stayed in jail forty days, and all the while new Freedom Riders were coming in every day.

Bernard: Did you ever have a fear of dying in the civil rights movement?

James: Oh, yes, yes. During much of the early sixties, I received threatening phone calls, though I was living in New York then, not in the Deep South. They called my home threatening my life, my wife, and my two daughters.

Bernard: Were you ever threatened by the KKK?

James: In fact, I was shot at by the Klan—the Ku Klux Klan in Bogalusa,

Louisiana. In Plaquemine, Louisiana, I had to escape from a lynch mob—that's a mob that's out to kill people, usually by hanging them. Those of us who were in a position of leadership knew that death might lurk around any corner.

Bernard: Do you think we'll ever be able to eliminate racism from this society?

James: I think so. Racism is the idea that skin color, hair texture, physical features, and so on have something to do with intelligence, character, and morality. We know that it's not true, yet people believe it. That prejudice, that belief that some races are superior and others are inferior, is racism. It is not innate—people are not born with it. Babies and small children don't have it. They develop it when it is taught to them by parents or by playmates in school. If it is a learned reaction, and I think it is, then it can be unlearned. We can stop teaching it to our children. If we stop teaching it, then racism will die a natural death.

Bernard: Thank you very much, Mr. Farmer, for your inspirational words.

Nicholas Osborne with Walter Fauntroy

Nicholas: This is Nicholas Osborne reporting live at New Bethel Baptist Church with Reverend Walter Fauntroy. Reverend Fauntroy, what was the most important thing you did in the civil rights movement?

Walter: Well, one of the things I did was help organize a nonviolent campaign in Birmingham, Alabama, at the Easter season in 1963, to help people all over the country see the unfairness of segregation.

Nicholas: What kinds of things did you do?

Walter: We started with sit-ins at lunch counters; then we marched on city hall. At that time, the police chief in Birmingham was a man by the name of Bull Connor. Now, can you think of why he was called that?

Nicholas: Because he got really mad?

Walter: Yes, and he was really stubborn—"bullheaded" is the term— and he decided that we were not going to be allowed to have what the First Amendment guarantees every citizen, and that is the right to "petition the government for redress of a grievance." That means that every one of us, black and white, has the right to ask the government to change something that is wrong.

Police spray civil rights activists with high-pressure fire hoses, which are strong enough to knock adults to the ground. This method was also used against children and teenagers who marched in Birmingham in May 1963. So many young people marched that the Birmingham struggle became known as the Children's Crusade.

Nicholas: And Bull Connor tried to stop you?

Walter: He beat us with billy clubs and knocked us down with fire hoses. And do you know what else? There were hundreds of children who tried to march through the city to protest segregation, and the police attacked and arrested them, too.

Nicholas: Kids? They attacked kids?

Walter: Yes, but they did it in front of

television cameras that took it to millions of people who agreed with us that segregation needed to be changed. You could say Birmingham pricked this country's conscience and made people put pressure on Congress, although it was a year before a law was passed.

Nicholas: Okay. One more question. What inspired you personally to become active in the civil rights movement?

Walter: Like Martin Luther King, I am a minister, and in the Bible, in the sixty-first chapter of the Book of Isaiah, it says—

Nicholas: Could you read me what it says?

Walter: I can tell you what it says, because the message is written in my heart: The spirit of the Lord God is upon me, because he hath anointed me to preach the Gospel to the poor, to bind up the brokenhearted, and to set at liberty them that are bound. And "Gospel" means "good news," did you know that?

Nicholas: I think so.

Walter: So when Dr. King and I and all the other ministers asked ourselves, "What is the good news the people in our churches want to hear?" our answer was, It would be good news if the "whites only" signs came down and black people were not humiliated every day by laws that said they were different from and less than other people.

Nicholas: Thank you for your time, Reverend Fauntroy.

Taniza Holmes with Dorothy Peyton

Taniza: My name is Taniza, and I'm here with my grandmother talking about marches and protests. Grandma, did you participate in any marches and protests?

Dorothy: Yes, I did.

Taniza: Which one? The March on Washington?

Dorothy: No, I wasn't there for that one, but I did march with Martin Luther King in the early sixties. I was marching in the front, right behind Dr. King. Block after block, we were joined by more marchers. The crowd became excited, and they were walking faster, and they surged forward, pushing the people in my row forward, causing me to step continuously on Dr. Martin Luther King's heels. I kept saying, "Excuse me, sir, excuse me, sir," all the way to the park where we were congregating.

Taniza: Did he get mad at you?

Dorothy: No, he was so nice and understanding. I'll never forget his smile. Dr. King meant a lot to me. I looked up to him and respected him so much and would have followed him anywhere.

Taniza: Well, he might not have liked

The white shoes of Dorothy Peyton can be seen to the left behind Martin Luther King, Jr., during a 1965 march to support elected government for Washington, D.C. Walter Fauntroy marches beside King.

that very much, Grandma, with you stepping on his heels.

Dorothy: I guess maybe you're right.

Taniza: Thank you, Grandma.

Dorothy: You're very welcome.

Latoya Thomas *with* Lawrence Still

Latoya: This is Latoya Thomas interviewing Lawrence Still. All right. Did you go to the March on Washington in 1963?

Lawrence: I did.

Latoya: How did you like it?

Lawrence: It was a wonderful surprise.

Latoya: What do you mean?

Lawrence: Well, when the march was being planned, we didn't know what was going to happen. You have to think back and remember that all of this was new. There were all kinds of projections about how many people would come, but there was always this concern, this fear, that it might not come off.

Latoya: Do you mean like a party when you buy chips and soda and sit around waiting for everyone to come, and then you start thinking maybe no one will?

Lawrence: Well, yes, kind of like that.

Latoya: But the people came.

Lawrence: Yes, they did. They were pouring over the bridges into Washington. They came in buses and trains. We saw cars and license plates

from all parts of the country. And this was even before we entered the city. There were people lining the streets, in every doorway, on every sidewalk, singing and waving. There were people from all over the world marching for justice.

Latoya: Did you hear Dr. King give his "I Have a Dream" speech?

Lawrence: Yes. And I'll tell you something not many people know. Much of what Dr. King said in his "I Have a Dream" speech was not in his written text.

Latoya: You mean he made it up, right there, in front of all those people?

Lawrence: He was, you might say, speaking from the heart. He knew how to give his lesson, to always preach to the people. He was eloquent.

Latoya: Do you think Dr. King felt he had arrived at his dream?

Lawrence: I don't think he expected it to be accomplished in his lifetime, but I think he did believe that he was well on the way.

August 28, 1963: A civil rights demonstrator at the March on Washington. Signs above her state one of the goals of the march: to persuade Congress to pass a civil rights law ending segregation.

Martin Luther King, Jr., giving his "I Have a Dream" speech at the March on Washington.

Latoya: What do you think of his dream? Do you think it can happen?

Lawrence: His dream essentially was Christ's dream, and Mahatma Gandhi's dream, and I think it will be fulfilled, not only for African Americans, but for all people.

Latoya: Well, I think so, too. Thank you.

Zachary Gittens with Jennifer Lawson and Tony Gittens

Zachary: Three, two, one. My name is Zachary Gittens, and I will be interviewing Jennifer Lawson, my mother. How long were you in the civil rights movement?

Jennifer: From the time I was sixteen until I was twenty-six.

Zachary: Did you work in any civil rights organizations?

Jennifer: Yes, I did. I worked in an organization called SNCC.

Zachary: Were you ever in a sit-in?

Jennifer: Yes, yes. I participated in one in Montgomery, the capital city of Alabama, in the early part of 1965. There were a few dozen of us, mostly students from Tuskegee University, and we held a sit-in on the steps of the capitol building to ask that Alabama remove restrictions that made it difficult for blacks to vote. And it was quite frightening because the police were on one side of us, but the Ku Klux Klan was on the other side, and they were threatening to kill us. And I was actually glad when the police arrested us.

Zachary: You got arrested?

Jennifer: Yes. We had vowed to be non-violent, and when the police came to arrest us, we'd do what they called "go

1961: Protesters in Savannah, Georgia, lock arms and go limp. They are about to be arrested for "nonviolent direct action." Protesters confronted segregation head-on, not only by demonstrating but also by allowing themselves to be arrested, and often not posting bail, to emphasize their commitment to justice and freedom.

limp." You just lay down, and the police would carry you and throw you into the wagon and take you off to jail. And so I spent a week in jail in Montgomery, Alabama.

Zachary: If you were a college student, how could you do all your homework and fight in the civil rights movement?

Jennifer: That was really difficult, and I had to make one of the hardest deci-

sions in my life. My family was poor, but I had gotten a scholarship to study science, and I was hoping to become a doctor. But I thought about it really hard, and I didn't want to be in a country where I couldn't go to restaurants or schools because of the color of my skin. I thought I could always go back to college, but this was a time when our country was ready to change. So I left in the middle of my junior year to work full-time in the civil rights movement.

Zachary: Thanks, Mom. Now I have some questions for Tony Gittens, my father. How long were you in the civil rights movement?

Tony: From 1965 through 1975, about ten years.

Zachary: What kind of work were you active in?

Tony: I was involved in trying to reform the educational system to educate African Americans about their own history and their own contributions to the United States and the world.

Zachary: Did you like what you did in the civil rights movement?

Tony: I don't know if "like" is the right way to put it. We learned a lot about working hard, taking a stand, and how to be a leader even though you don't feel comfortable being a leader, because someone has to do it. We learned how to work with people even if you didn't totally like everything they said or did, how to trust each other. What made it worth doing is that we helped improve the situation in the United States for African Americans and for all people.

Jennifer: What I hope you would learn from Dad's and my experience is that people, even high school and college students, can stand up for justice and freedom. We were able to make a change in our country.

Zachary: Thank you. This concludes my interview with my parents.

Tony Gittens (right) listens to another student during a demonstration at Howard University in 1967.

Kionna Brooks with Maurice Sorrell

Kionna: Mr. Sorrell, were you a professional photographer during the civil rights movement?

Maurice: Yes, I was a photographer for *Ebony* magazine, and I was sent to the South to cover this great event.

Kionna: Where did you take pictures?

Maurice: I photographed the march from Selma to Montgomery, Alabama, to demand equal voting rights for African Americans. Since the first group of marchers was beaten, the government sent down federal marshals for protection. As we got near Montgomery, I was afraid that a white mob was going to break through the line of marshals.

Kionna: But you didn't have to worry. You were a photographer, not a demonstrator.

Maurice: To many people, being a black photographer was worse. I was a black person in a position of power, and that's an obvious target. I even had to ride in the back of a hearse—the limousine they carry dead people in—so I wouldn't be seen riding through the southern cities.

Kionna: What was the saddest thing you saw?

Maurice: Well, you know, Kionna,

HEAR!   HEAR!
HOW OUR BROTHERS
Died For Freedom
AND HOW WE ARE CARRYING
ON THE FIGHT IN MISSISSIPPI

Mickey Schwerner   James Chaney   Andrew Goodman

HEAR
Mrs. Fanny Chaney
Courageous Mother of James Chaney
At New Zion Baptist Church
2319 THIRD STREET
THURS., AUG. 27, 1964
7:30 P. M.
CORE

This flyer with photos of the recently murdered CORE workers Michael Schwerner, James Chaney, and Andrew Goodman invites Mississippians to a meeting honoring them.

many people gave their lives for the struggle for civil rights, not just Martin Luther King but regular volunteers, both white and black. The saddest thing I had to do was to cover the death of James Chaney for the magazine. Chaney was one of three civil rights workers killed in Neshoba County, Mississippi, while they were trying to register African American voters. The other two were Andrew Goodman and Michael Schwerner. They later made a movie about the event called *Mississippi Burning*. I was there at the funeral with Mr. Chaney's mother. It was a very sad day.

Kionna: Do you think the people who died were sorry they ever got mixed up in the whole movement?

Maurice: No, I'm sure if they had to do it all over again, they would have done the very same thing. Sometimes you have to make a stand for what's right, even if it means risking your life.

Kionna: Thank you, Mr. Sorrell.

Asa Fager with Charles Fager

Asa: Hi. This is Asa Fager. I'm interviewing my dad, Chuck Fager. Dad, did you participate in the civil rights movement at all?

Charles: Yes, I did. As a matter of fact, I knew Dr. Martin Luther King, Jr.

Asa: No way.

Charles: You knew that.

Asa: I know, but I'm pretending that I'm just the interviewer. Tell me about how you met Dr. King, Dad.

Charles: Well, in late 1964, I started working with Dr. King. He was getting ready to start a campaign in Selma, Alabama. He wanted to put pressure on the federal government to pass a law to make it possible for black people to vote in the South.

Asa: Did you have any marches in Selma?

Charles: Well, the Selma campaign was about three months long. There were a few different marches that took place. We marched from a church called Brown's Chapel Church downtown to the county courthouse. And the sheriff, Jim Clark, didn't like us to stand around his courthouse. So, many people got arrested.

Asa: Did you?

Charles: Yes.

Asa: Can you tell me about it?

Charles: Well, I got arrested with Dr. King and about 250 other people. They took us to the county jail. We made a lot of noise, singing and clapping, and sometimes we'd hear the women on the other side of the jail singing and stomping their feet. They'd make the whole place shake. It was really kind of exciting.

Asa: Was Dr. King very upset to be put in jail?

Charles: Well, jail for Dr. King was like a vacation, because every day there were people wanting him to do things, and he had to make speeches all the time. He seldom got any time to himself. So when he went to jail, he always tried to take his friend Ralph Abernathy with him. He was another minister who worked for civil rights. It was what they called going on retreat, where you go off for a while and sit quietly and think and read and pray.

Asa: Did you demonstrate again when you got out of jail?

Charles: Yes. I was there when we made our first attempt to march from Selma to Montgomery. When the marchers tried to cross the bridge outside the city, a bunch of troopers and deputies attacked with clubs and whips and tear gas, and chased people back across the river.

Asa: How did you feel when you saw people being beat up?

Charles: It was frightening, it was unbelievable, and people got very angry. When they finally got back to the church where the march had started, many of them were so upset they wanted to get guns and fight back. I was running around with a few other people saying, "Please go back in, please calm down. Remember, they've got more guns than you'll ever get."

Asa: And did they go back into the church?

Charles: Yes, eventually.

Asa: Dad, someday will you take me to the South and show me all these places you talk about?

Charles: You know, Asa, that's a great idea. I'm going to take you down to Selma, and to Atlanta, where Dr. King is buried, and maybe up to Tennessee where he was killed. And you can see these places—because, you know, it was important to me personally, but it was also important to the country. It changed America through the power of nonviolence.

Asa: Thanks, Dad.

March 7, 1965: SNCC's John Lewis (right) and the Reverend Hosea Williams (left) lead the first voting rights march from Selma to Montgomery. Despite what the billboard in the background states, not everyone was welcome in Selma. Minutes after this photo was taken, Alabama troopers attacked the demonstrators.

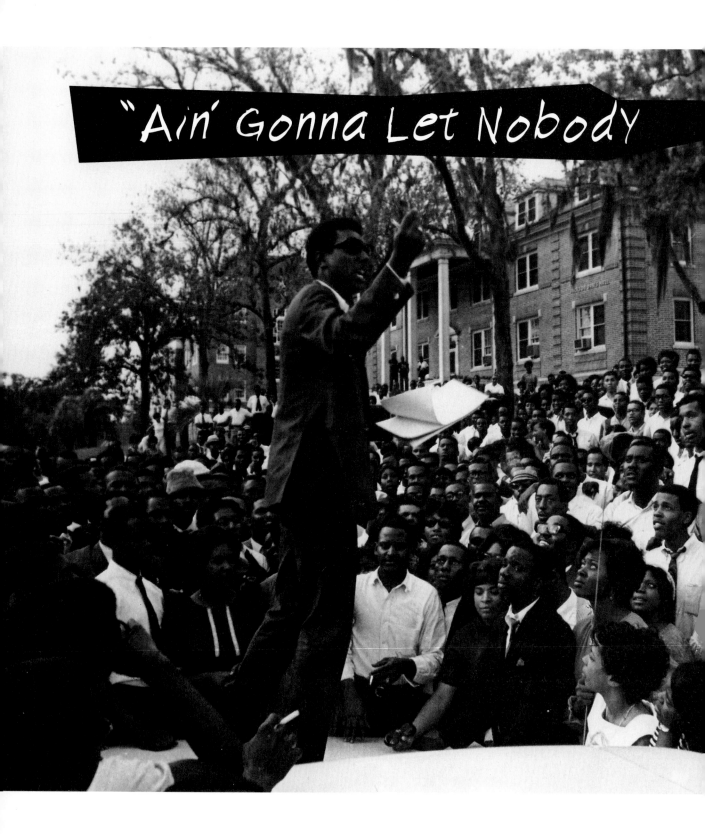

"Ain' Gonna Let Nobody

"Turn Me 'Round"

The Movement Shifts: The Struggle to End Poverty and Discrimination

On June 16, 1966, a young man named Stokely Carmichael stood before a group of tired civil rights marchers in Greenwood, Mississippi. He was the head of SNCC, and he was angry because he had been arrested for not leaving a building at the order of the police. Carmichael raised his fist in the air and shouted, "This is the twenty-seventh time I have been arrested—and I ain't going to jail no more! . . . We been saying freedom for six years and we ain't got nothin'. What we gonna start saying now is Black Power! . . . That's right, that's what we want. . . . From now on, when they ask you what you want, you know what to tell them. What do you want?"

Standing on the hood of a car at Florida A & M University in Tallahassee, Stokely Carmichael, head of SNCC, speaks to students about Black Power.

"Black Power!" the crowd yelled.

"What do you want? Say it again!"

"Black Power! Black Power! Black Power!"

Although Carmichael was the first to proclaim it as a strategy before a crowd of nonviolent protesters, Black Power was not a new idea. It was embodied in every effort black people made to gain freedom and respect, and had been articulated by black leaders since slavery. In the late nineteenth century, when Bishop Benjamin Tanner of the African Methodist Episcopal Church encouraged black people to advance themselves economically by developing businesses, he was expressing Black Power. When Marcus Garvey formed black military units in the 1920s, he was expressing Black Power. The New Negro Movement of the 1930s expressed Black Power by creating art and literature that did not copy white ideas of beauty or value.

Black Power was a way of thinking that encouraged African Americans to rely on themselves rather than on white people to change their lives and communities. It called for African Americans to be proud of themselves and their African heritage. It rejected the idea that black people were inferior and needed to act or look more "white"—to fit into white society—to be successful.

In the 1950s and 1960s, Black Power found a voice in the Nation of Islam, a Black Muslim group headed by Elijah Muhammad. At the same time that protesters were fighting for integration in the South, the Nation offered another solution to injustice and inequality: separate government, police force, schools, and businesses for African Americans. Many in the Nation believed that whites were "devils" who would never allow African Americans true equality, even if segregation ended.

Malcolm X, one of the Nation's most charismatic leaders, brought this message to the people. On street corners, on television, on college campuses, he proclaimed that the only way for blacks to be strong, independent, and equal was to live separate-

Elijah Muhammad (left), who brought the Nation of Islam to prominence in the 1950s and 1960s, and his most famous minister, Malcolm X.

ly. He spoke about achieving equality and justice "by any means necessary." Malcolm X articulated the anger of a people who had been denied their rights and treated with disrespect for hundreds of years.

In the 1960s, an increasing number of African Americans were attracted by Malcolm X's words and by the idea of Black Power. They were frustrated because the end of legal segregation did not mean equality. Many black people continued to suffer from poverty and discrimination, without educational opportunities, adequate health care, or decent jobs and homes. The civil rights movement as a whole was beginning to focus more on these problems, but people were divided about the best way to solve them.

By the mid-1960s, SNCC members like Stokely Carmichael were growing impatient with the Southern Christian Leadership Conference and the NAACP. They felt these groups were too quick to compromise with the government and to appease white people who were upset with the pace of change. Their experiences in the front lines of the movement—registering voters in the Deep South—had also made them angry. They had been beaten and jailed so many times that they questioned the strategy of nonviolent protest and wanted to start fighting back when they were attacked. SNCC became more militant—openly

A poster displayed by CORE members in Harlem, New York City, calls for black people to achieve power by helping each other and themselves.

1969: New York store owners modeling "Afro-American" fashions sold in their store.

aggressive, more combative in style—and embraced the ideals of Black Power: self-reliance, self-respect, and self-defense.

They were not alone. Black Power seemed to sweep the country, expressing itself in many ways. Tired of learning about their own heritage as a topic within "white" American history, black high school and college students began to demand classes that taught black and African history and achievements. In celebration of their heritage, African Americans traded in their jackets and ties for dashikis—long, loose-fitting, brightly patterned pullover shirts worn by many people in Africa. They stopped straightening their hair with chemicals to look more "white" and began wearing it in a natural style called an Afro. Slogans like "Black is beautiful" and "Say it loud! I'm black and I'm proud" captured the spirit of the time.

Black Power was also a way to support African American communities and defend them from neglect, discrimination, and racial violence. The Black Panthers, founded by Huey P. Newton and Bobby Seale in 1966, worked in black urban neighborhoods all over the country.

To protect themselves in case of attack, the Panthers exercised the right to "keep and bear arms"—own and carry weapons—described in the Second Amendment to the Constitution. This was in response to harassment from the police and frequent arrests of black people, particularly young black men. Panthers were attacked, jailed, and killed in FBI and police campaigns to destroy the group.

Although the Black Panthers received much publicity for their militant behavior, they also helped their communities by serving free breakfasts to kids, providing clothes and shoes to those who needed them, and offering classes to teach blacks how to defend themselves in court. Unfortunately, most people associated the Panthers with guns; few even knew about the breakfast programs.

Although groups like the Panthers were responding to white violence against them, many newspaper and television stories emphasized *their* "violence." In fact, both militant and nonviolent civil rights activists worked against random violence, trying to counter the rage and despair in poor black communities.

Nonetheless, some of that rage exploded in the summer of 1965, when a crowd of bystanders in Watts, a black neighborhood of Los Angeles, California, argued with police, who were about to arrest a young black man. California had no history of legal segregation, yet Watts was plagued by poverty and hopelessness. Of the 250,000 black people living there in 1965, two thirds depended on welfare. Only five of the 205 police officers serving Watts were African Americans, and, as in other cities, the police and the black community had a history of tension and mistrust.

The dispute over this one arrest in Watts set off a six-day riot, and by the time it ended, thirty-four people had died, nine hundred had been injured, and property damage had soared past

Black Panther member Brad Jones serves breakfast to hungry kids at the organization's Philadelphia headquarters in 1970.

$200 million. The anger continued to build; in 1966 and 1967, black people rioted in more than a hundred American cities.

Although people tended to lump together the rioters and the more militant civil rights activists, they were very different. Riots destroyed the same neighborhoods that militant groups wanted to improve, and rioting was not something that led to self-respect, equality, or true change. Nevertheless, many Americans were frightened by the militant style itself, at a time when they were just getting used to nonviolent protesters marching in their

Chicago, April 8, 1968:
A business district is devastated by arsonists and looters during the riots following the assassination of Martin Luther King, Jr.

Sunday best. They associated violence with the protests of the late 1960s.

As 1968 began, the fight against discrimination and poverty continued, but with less widespread support than for the fight against segregation. The focus of Americans had also turned from the civil rights movement to the movement against the war in Vietnam. The United States had sent troops to stop Communist North Vietnam from taking over South Vietnam, and Americans were dying. When people marched on Washington now, they marched against American involvement in Vietnam. Some black leaders, including Martin Luther King, Jr., and Stokely Carmichael, spoke out against the war.

In addition to their antiwar efforts, activists still worked to improve the lives of black people. In March, King went to Memphis, Tennessee, to support striking sanitation workers who wanted the city to recognize their union. On April 4, 1968, as he stood on a motel balcony just before dinnertime, he was shot to death by a sniper with a high-powered rifle from across the street.

Within hours, African Americans in more than sixty cities across the country were rioting, enraged by the violent death of a man who had dedicated himself to nonviolence. Entire neighborhoods turned into war zones overnight. Fires burned and smoldered as the riots continued for days, fueled by grief and anguish.

Historians often talk about "watershed" years. A watershed in nature is a ridge of high land that divides flowing water into two different rivers. In history, it is a turning point in the flow of events and the way a people think about their country. Many who write about American history consider 1968 to have been a watershed year. Demonstrations both for civil rights and against the Vietnam War had grown more militant. In the early 1960s, most people had understood and even supported the demonstrators, but now they felt the demonstrations had gone too far, creating too much unrest. An increasing number of Americans called

for the return of "law and order," wanting the police and government to stop demonstrations of all kinds.

In this atmosphere, the civil rights movement seemed to lose momentum. Its two most famous leaders had been assassinated: Malcolm X in 1965 and Martin Luther King, Jr., in 1968. The movement was struggling against something more complicated than legal segregation—poverty and discrimination—and the Vietnam War was draining resources and energy from this effort. And violence, whether from riots or police attacks, made the fight for change even more difficult.

But these setbacks do not tarnish the genuine accomplishments of the civil rights movement. Whether nonviolent or militant, demonstrators did something that would have seemed impossible fifty years ago: they ended segregation; they provided opportunities for black people in education, work, and politics; and they instilled a pride and self-respect in being African American. In the 1950s and 1960s, the United States took a giant leap toward realizing the ideals of justice and equality. It was a time to be proud of.

Today, the same issues that once confronted the civil rights movement continue to challenge Americans. They struggle not only for civil—legal—rights, but for the human right to respect, to decent homes and health care, and to opportunities in jobs and education. This struggle includes people of all races and backgrounds: Latinos, Native Americans, and Asian Americans who have suffered from discrimination, as well as European Americans and African Americans. It has grown to embrace the international struggle for civil and human rights in countries like South Africa, China, and El Salvador.

Everyone can work to achieve this goal: to treat all human beings with a single standard of courtesy, decency, and fairness, regardless of their color, their gender, or their beliefs. In doing so, we guarantee our own rights and dignity, and build a better world.

April 5, 1995: Latinos demonstrate at the U.S. Capitol for affordable, adequate health care for everyone.

Catherine Osborne with Ethel Minor

Catherine: Ms. Minor, how did you first get involved with the Nation of Islam?

Ethel: I had just returned to Chicago after living in Colombia, South America.

Catherine: Excuse me, but why were you in South America?

Ethel: A good question. I think I was trying to escape from a country that offered me limited opportunities. I wanted to work at the United Nations, but when I got my degree in 1959, the U.S. government was not hiring "colored girls" to represent this country.

Catherine: But in the 1960s there were all those sit-ins and marches going on. Why didn't you just take part in them?

Ethel: I saw that as people who were in an inferior position begging to be let in by people who were in a superior position. "Master, will you please let me come in and eat a hamburger in your store, let me drink out of your water fountain?" I found that very humiliating.

Catherine: But you did come back to the United States.

Ethel: Yes, in 1962, and that's when I saw Malcolm X on television. He was explaining the program of the Honorable Elijah Muhammad, who founded the Nation of Islam. Malcolm was like a truth-bearing angel from heaven. There he was on the white man's television, "telling it like it is."

Catherine: And that's when you got involved?

Ethel: Yes, I went over to Muhammad's Mosque Number Two in Chicago, knocked on the door with no appointment or anything, and said, "I want to know more about this." Then I went to hear the Honorable Elijah Muhammad speak at a large auditorium.

Catherine: What was it like being there?

Ethel: It was electrifying. The Muslim men walked around holding their heads up high. I had never seen black men act the way they did. They were proud, they were in charge. They were very courteous to me and the friend I was

with, who happened to be white.

Catherine: What did the Honorable Elijah Muhammad talk about?

Ethel: He talked about why the "American Negroes" were in such an inferior situation. He always called us the "so-called American Negro," saying that America was not our country and we didn't even know our real names. Since we had been forced to take on the slave masters' names, we should proudly adopt the "X" as a symbol of our true names. He also said we would never have equality in America. Since we were obviously a "problem," he proposed that we ask the former slave masters for some land where we could build a separate nation. It didn't mean we wanted to fight white folks. Maybe they would even grant us foreign aid. They

Black Muslim women and their sons walk to their mosque, an Islamic house of worship, in Washington, D.C. Black Muslims are followers of Islam, a religion practiced by many Africans.

were sure giving other folks a lot of foreign aid—why not include the former slaves?

Catherine: That surprises me.

Ethel: Why?

Catherine: Because I always thought the civil rights movement struggled to get black and white people together, not keep them separate.

Ethel: Well, the civil rights movement worked for equality and justice, and there were many strategies to achieve that. Many of us were impressed by the Honorable Elijah Muhammad's analysis of the race problem in this country. He was a very intelligent man with a quick wit. I remember him saying, "To get a man off his knees, you have to tell him he's superior, not that he's just as good as white people. If you tell him he's just as good, he may never get up. Tell him he's superior and maybe, just maybe, he'll stand up, even hold his head up high."

Catherine: Thank you so much for talking to me about these things, Ms. Minor.

Ethel Minor (second from right) and other teachers at the University of Islam in Chicago listen to Malcolm X speak in 1963.

Hakiba and Janali Thompson with Akili Ron Anderson

Janali: This is Janali Thompson. I'm here with my brother, Hakiba, interviewing Akili Ron Anderson, and I will ask the first question. Do you remember the civil rights movement?

Akili: Yes, and it was a great movement symbolized by Martin Luther King, Jr. But do you know, in the middle of the 1960s there were other movements that were like the civil rights movement, but which disagreed with the policy of nonviolence. There was a whole group of us who were saying, "Look, we are prepared to defend ourselves not just for freedom but to live in peace." And many of us didn't believe that integration was the answer.

Janali: What's wrong with integration?

Akili: We thought that we could be part of this country as different nations of people, but to have to sit beside a white child in school to be successful was not necessary. It would be nice if you wanted to, if they wanted to, but we weren't going to force ourselves or move into a white neighborhood where people wanted to burn crosses in our yards.

Janali: You said that it was okay to be "different nations of people." What do you mean?

Akili: Do you know what a nation is?

Hakiba: A lot of people in one place?

Akili: A nation is a group of people who have a common history and a common destiny. This country has many "nations," many nationalities. There are Italian Americans and Chinese Americans who are a nation within this country, with their own customs and their own neighborhoods. Somebody who celebrates his nation or himself is a nationalist. I'm a black nationalist. Why?

Hakiba: Because you live in a black neighborhood?

Akili: Yes. I want to be in a black neighborhood. I want my children to go to a black school. I want to buy from black shop owners. I want to support my community first.

Akiba: Is that why you paint black people in your pictures?

Akili: Yes; as an artist, I am inspired by you. When I say "you," I mean our people. Nothing I could think of comes anywhere close to the majesty of who we are. But you know, it was only in high school that I reached a point of understanding that I could paint black people. In junior high— I'm serious—I didn't realize I could.

Hakiba: How about in elementary school?

Akili: In elementary school, I always painted all-white images, because that's what you saw. All the dolls were white, the pictures in books were white. And when I finally did start depicting black people, I felt a little uncomfortable. I was afraid that somebody would say, "Well, what do you think you're doing?" Then I realized, as they said in the 1960s, that "black *is* beautiful."

Janali and Hakiba: What did "black is beautiful" mean?

Akili: It meant that we, as African people, had finally decided that black was not ugly. Because that's what we thought. But then we were no longer brainwashed to believe we were ugly. We were not only physically beautiful, we were spiritually beautiful. We were beautiful because we knew our history. We understood why our skin is like it is, why our lips are like they are, why we dance, why we run, how we think. We were beautiful because we were proud of ourselves.

Janali: My brother and I thank you for answering our questions.

Rashida Holman with Yuri Kochiyama

Rashida: My name is Rashida, and I'm in Harlem, New York, interviewing my great-aunt Yuri. What problems did you encounter that helped you realize the importance of civil rights?

Yuri: In 1941, when Japan bombed Pearl Harbor, the U.S. declared war on Japan. And every person of Japanese ancestry in California, Oregon, and Washington was sent to concentration camps just because their background was Japanese.

Rashida: Even though you were an American citizen? That's terrible.

Yuri: Yes, and it was very hard. The camps were located in the desert, or mountains, or salt flats, or swamplands. The climate was very harsh. We were confined to a one-mile enclosure. We had all our civil rights taken away.

Rashida: Is that how an Asian American got involved in an issue that the public thought was a black-and-white issue?

Yuri: Do you mean the civil rights movement? Well, many people were in the civil rights movement. It was really a rainbow color of people who participated throughout the fifties and sixties.

Rashida: How did you manage to get involved with Malcolm X?

Yuri: In 1963, I was arrested for demonstrating to get more construction jobs for black people. And when I was at city court, who should be there but Malcolm X. Because I wasn't black, I didn't know if I should try to talk to him. But I went closer to him, and there was a moment that he looked up and saw me, and he probably wondered what this old Asian woman was doing there. I said, "Malcolm, can I shake your hand?" And he said, "What for?" And I said, "Oh, I want to congratulate you." And he said, "For what?" And I said, "For what you are doing for your people." And he said, "What am I doing for my people?" And I said, "You're giving them direction." And then all of a sudden, he gave a big smile, and came forward, and we shook hands.

Rashida: Is that the only time you spoke to him?

Yuri: No. I wrote him several times, but he never wrote back. Then, in January 1964, I got a letter from a Japanese peace mission, and they wanted to talk to Malcolm more than any other figure in America. I invited Malcolm to a reception on June 6. We had a black folk singer and a Japanese classical singer, and all the black civil rights leaders from Harlem and some white activists. They all gathered at my apartment, but none of us knew whether Malcolm was really going to show.

Rashida: Well, did he?

Yuri: In the middle of the reception, someone knocked on the door, and it was Malcolm.

Rashida: I still can't believe you knew him. What was he like?

Yuri: There were no Muslims there, and people wondered if he would be cold to such a crowd. But he was warm and gracious. He shook hands with every single person, and he was as warm to the white people as he was to the black people. People noticed that right away. It was, for us, a historic moment, because Asians had never had an opportunity to meet him. And the first thing he said to me was "I apologize for never writing to you. If I go anywhere again, I will write to you." Later he sent me eleven postcards when he traveled.

Rashida: When was the last time you saw Malcolm X?

Yuri: The last time that we all saw Malcolm was February 21, 1965, the day he was killed. And it was at the Audubon Ballroom, where he always had his meetings.

Rashida: Where was the Audubon Ballroom?

Yuri: It's located on 166th Street and Broadway in New York City. On that day I think everybody felt something was going to happen.

Rashida: Why?

Yuri: None of the people who were asked to speak had showed up. And a couple of weeks before, Malcolm's home was bombed. The last week, he didn't even stay with his family, because he wanted to safeguard them.

Rashida: So what happened on that day?

Yuri: Malcolm came onstage to speak, and then there was a distraction in the middle of the room. One guy yelled, "Get your hands off my pocket!" and then another guy started arguing. Of course, everybody was looking at the distraction. Then, all of a sudden, the shots rang out, and when we

February 21, 1965: The body of Malcolm X is carried from the Audubon Ballroom, where he was fatally shot.

looked back, it was already too late.

Rashida: What did people do? What was happening?

Yuri: It was just utter pandemonium. All the chairs came crashing down, there was screaming and yelling. Someone came past me, running up to the stage, so I just followed. I just went right to where Malcolm had fallen and put his head on my lap, hoping that he was going to come to.

Rashida: How did you feel?

Yuri: Everybody was just shocked. Later, when I got on the subway—I had to go to work that day—it came over the subway loudspeaker that Malcolm X was dead. And people couldn't believe it. I couldn't believe it. But I think it was true to the struggle in a way. I think it made people even more aware that this was what the struggle was about. That it was serious, really serious. And after that, the movement became much more militant.

Rashida: Thank you, Aunt Yuri, for telling us your story.

Menelik Coates with Paul Coates

Menelik: Hello. I am Menelik Paul Cabron Coates, with my father, Mr. Coates. Mr. Coates, where and when were you in the Black Panther party?

Paul: I was in the Baltimore chapter from 1969 through 1971.

Menelik: What did you do?

Paul: I was the defense captain.

Menelik: You mean you were in charge of all the guns?

Paul: Actually, Menelik, the Panthers rarely carried guns openly. We always had guns in our homes because, as we saw it, the black community was constantly under attack, particularly by police. So what we needed at the time was a force to defend ourselves and our communities, but not just with guns. Part of defense was setting up programs to make the community strong and provide the basic necessities. The Panthers had free clothing and shoe programs, free food programs . . .

Menelik: Like the stuff they do for homeless people now?

Paul: Well, this was in the 1960s, before homelessness was so noticeable, so setting up programs that fed people for free was a really big thing. It was a way of pointing out that America underserved black people, particularly black children.

Menelik: Were there people in the Black Panther party you admired?

Paul: I admired Huey P. Newton, the

founder of the party. Black people were used to histories in which there weren't heroes who stood up against white oppression, so for Huey P. Newton to stand up and call the police pigs . . .

Menelik: He really said that?

Paul: He really did. And to tell the police, "If you shoot another black person, I'm shooting you, and if I don't beat you with the gun, I'll beat you with the lawbook"—for a black person to do that and *survive* was very, very heroic.

Menelik: Could you explain about beating them with the lawbook?

Paul: Black people's rights in the courts were not protected, so we held political and legal education classes so the community would become knowledgeable about the law. In fact, the Panthers followed ten principles taken directly from the Bill of Rights, like the right to bear arms and the right of free speech. These are traditional American values, guaranteed by the Constitution. You see, we didn't have a problem living under America's laws, if those laws could be applied fairly and equally.

Menelik: At one time, though, would the Panthers actually go kill policemen if a policeman killed a black person?

Paul: You did have shoot-outs between Panthers and police, but most of it was police setting up and shooting Panthers, even though the Panthers got the rap for it. See, the Panthers used rhetoric to avoid shooting.

Menelik: What's rhetoric?

Baltimore, 1971: Paul Coates speaks at Black Panther headquarters where a press conference is taking place to expose a police agent.

Black Panthers march in New York City in July 1968 to protest murder charges brought against Huey P. Newton in Oakland, California. They believed Newton's imprisonment was part of an organized campaign by the government to destroy the Black Panthers.

Paul: What we call fat mouthing. The Panthers were masters of the threat, about "what we gonna do." A lot of the Panthers came off the street, and they knew that a lot of times you don't have to fight if you tell people, "I'm gonna kick your butt. If you cross me, I'm gonna hurt you." That's all you have to say. The ability to use words has great power in the black community.

Menelik: Is that like Black Power?

Paul: Menelik, Black Power is the ability of black people to think for themselves, to speak for themselves, and to do for themselves. People use the term to talk about the movements of the 1960s, but black people have always struggled for Black Power. Early on, it manifested itself in a resistance to slavery. In the civil rights time, it manifested itself in the struggle for the right to vote. Black Power is a force for equalizing. It's not about blacks wanting to be superior or to treat anyone badly. It's simply a way for us to be equal in this world.

Menelik: Okay. Thanks, Dad—I mean, Mr. Coates.

Elliot Tarloff with Erik Tarloff

Elliot: Dad, were you ever in any demonstrations?

Erik: Yes.

Elliot: Okay. What exactly were they about?

Erik: The one that was the most dramatic was at the University of California at Berkeley, where there was a strike to start a black studies program.

Elliot: Strike?

Erik: Where students refuse to attend classes until the university agrees. I attended those rallies and demonstrations.

Elliot: Were other people involved in it?

Erik: No; the amazing thing was, I was the only person who showed up at those demonstrations.

Elliot: No, really.

Erik: Yes, many people were involved because it was such a big university and an important issue.

Elliot: Why did you get involved?

Erik: I thought there was justice in the demand that black studies be part of the curriculum.

Elliot: What's the curriculum?

A student strike at Howard University in the late 1960s. Student activists across the country demanded more black teachers, more black studies courses, and a voice in setting school policies.

Erik: What's taught in the classes. We didn't study things like the structure of black civilization and we didn't usually read black writers. This was a side of American history which was ignored except as it had influence on white people, and I didn't think that was right.

Elliot: So you didn't just demonstrate to get out of algebra class?

Erik: No. It didn't work that way at Berkeley anyway, because they never took attendance. But it *was* more exciting to be at a demonstration than to go to class.

Elliot: Did you want to take black studies?

Erik: It would have been interesting, but as I said, the reason I demonstrated was that it was part of American culture and it ought to be studied seriously. I did have mixed feelings about making it a separate program, which the black students wanted.

Elliot: Why?

Erik: I thought it could easily be part of American studies. To keep it separate seemed to bring back the segregation which we had all been against when it was forced on everybody by the white power structure. To suddenly have black radicals say, "We're entirely separate from the rest of the university and from your society" didn't seem constructive.

Elliot: But you demonstrated anyway?

Erik: Yes. On balance, I decided I was for it.

Elliot: Did you ever feel like those demonstrations weren't enough, that you wanted to do more?

Erik: No. I think all of us were amazed that we could actually have the impact on the university that we did. It was such a big institution, almost like a city. That we could actually bring it to a halt, that we had some ability to influence what was going on around us, was a major discovery. Do you have another question?

Elliot: No. Thank you for this interview, Dad.

Erik: Well, don't let it happen again.

Jonathan Botts with Marsha and Carlos Botts

Jonathan: Wednesday, September 8. I'm having a civil rights interview with my mother. Did you know about the riots after Martin Luther King was shot?

Marsha: Oh, yes. I was fourteen, and I can remember seeing the smoke from burning buildings come up the hill on Fourteenth Street in Washington, D.C., where we lived. You could see the smoke rise after so many hours of smoldering. But I also remember specifically when things had cooled down. It was Palm Sunday, and I was going to Sunday school on a Metrobus, and there weren't too many people in the streets. But when we got to Sixteenth and U, I remember seeing the National Guard standing on the corner guarding the street. I think that picture will always remain in my mind, to see them out there on Palm Sunday trying to keep law and order.

Jonathan: How did you feel about the riots?

Marsha: I was mystified. The riots were bad, but in my household what was even worse was that someone had killed the Dreamer. My parents felt that the rioting was foolish, it was not going to give us the results we were hoping for. And, indeed, we hurt ourselves more than we hurt the so-called enemy. But we felt more heartsick about Dr. King's death than we did about the rioting and loss of business.

Jonathan: Thanks, Mom. Now I'm interviewing my father about the civil rights era. Dad, did you or your family like Malcolm X better than Martin Luther King?

Carlos: My family thought they were all radical, but they could tolerate King better than Malcolm X. I've always personally felt closer to King because of my faith, but I have a great respect for Malcolm X. He was in the Muslim movement, but he didn't just get stuck there, he traveled and saw the bigger Islamic religion, and he had the guts to step out and say, "Wait a minute, we've been doing it wrong, we can work with people who aren't black." But back then, during the black consciousness movement, I was feeling more radical. I liked that Malcolm X would stand up and say, "We're not going to take no stuff." I identified with his anger, and I identified with his love for the black man, and for his thinking that we needed to concentrate on ourselves and our black culture, and not try to put so much energy into integrating, and trying to be where you're not wanted.

Jonathan: How did you feel about the riots after Dr. King died?

Carlos: It was a scary time. I was in junior high school, and we had one white classmate. We knew he could be in trouble, so we walked him home. We just knew that it might not be safe for him.

Jonathan: Mom said she saw the smoke burning. Did you actually see the riots?

Carlos: Yes. When I got home, my mom gave me the money she had in her purse and I ran to the store to buy things like milk and bread. I saw people running around the streets, hitting all the stores, acting crazy. And later, all the stores were closed. We would take our wagon and go to different churches that would give you food. My mom still had to work, and we'd surprise her because we would have all this different food when she got home. It was a crazy time, but it brought the neighborhood together, I think. We just had to get angry and grieve together.

Jonathan: Thanks, Dad, and you, too, Mom. This is Jonathan Botts. See you.

April 16, 1968: A National Guardsman enters a burned-out grocery store on 14th Street N.W. in Washington, D.C., to warn off would-be looters. The riots that followed Martin Luther King, Jr.'s death scarred dozens of American cities. Some neighborhoods have never been rebuilt.

Wilson Myers with Kathleen O'Neill

Wilson: This is Wilson Myers interviewing Mrs. O'Neill. Mrs. O'Neill, do you remember the day when Martin Luther King was killed?

Kathleen: Yes, I do remember that. It was a horrible day, and they showed the shots at the Lorraine Motel where he was killed on television. And then the riots started, and that was very scary. I was a nun, and I was teaching at a Catholic school outside Washington, D.C. We woke up in the morning and saw the National Guard surrounding our school. And we went outside, and they told us that down in the city, the whole Fourteenth Street corridor was in flames. As the days went on, we discovered that people were put out of their homes because of the fire.

Wilson: Since you were a nun, was it kind of your job to do something to help?

Kathleen: I think it was everybody's job, and many people did help. At the school we collected clothes and food. Then we had to get in a van and go downtown. And the only way you could get into downtown then without being shot at by a rioter or having a firebomb blown up in your face was if you wrote the word "soul," s-o-u-l, on the side of your van.

Wilson: Soul?

Kathleen: It was short for "soul brother" or "soul sister," which meant being part of the African American community or sympathetic to it. We wrote it, but we were still scared going in, because there were people around with guns, pointing them at us or shooting at the tires of our van. But we were determined to get that food and clothes to these people who were burned out of their houses.

Wilson: So did you make it?

Kathleen: We made it to St. Mary's Church right on Fourteenth Street,

In the aftermath of Dr. King's death, churches and other community groups distributed food and clothing to riot victims at emergency shelters. This center was housed in a church in Washington, D.C.

and we got it to the people, came back unharmed, and this went on for several days.

Wilson: What were your feelings about this time?

Kathleen: After the riots calmed down, we did a lot of soul-searching.

Wilson: Is that like soul brother or soul sister?

Kathleen: No, this is a different kind of soul. You look into your heart, really think about the way you've been acting. I was disappointed in myself, because up to this point, I hadn't thought about civil rights very much. And this made me very aware of it and made me want to change the way I was living and teaching, so that my students would understand the importance of equal rights. There is a saying: "If you want peace, work for justice." And I think that's true.

Wilson: Okay, that's all of it. Thank you, Mrs. O'Neill.

Maisha Williams *with* Tom Tarrants

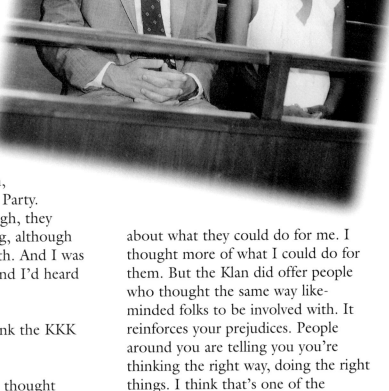

Maisha: This is Maisha Williams interviewing the Reverend Tom Tarrants. What is it that you do?

Tom: I am a minister in an interracial church, where people of all backgrounds worship together.

Maisha: But you weren't always a minister. You were in the Ku Klux Klan, right? What made you decide to join the Ku Klux Klan?

Tom: Well, actually, I'd been involved in another racist organization, the National States Rights Party. They weren't violent enough, they professed to be law-abiding, although that wasn't exactly the truth. And I was much more radical then, and I'd heard about the Klan.

Maisha: What did you think the KKK could do for you?

Tom: I'm not sure I really thought about what they could do for me. I thought more of what I could do for them. But the Klan did offer people who thought the same way like-minded folks to be involved with. It reinforces your prejudices. People around you are telling you you're thinking the right way, doing the right things. I think that's one of the reasons a lot of people join, in addition to the fact that they're attracted by the ideology, the hatred of blacks and Jews, and getting simple answers to a lot of complicated questions.

Maisha: Why were you against these races and religions?

Tom: I didn't start off against anyone, but during the civil rights movement in the South, they began integrating the public schools in Alabama, where I was raised. Everything was in turmoil because a whole way of life was being overturned. And the Klan and other racist groups came along with a simple answer. I don't believe any of it now, but in those days, I was very alarmed by integration. And the Klan creates a kind of crisis mentality. You feel you've got to do something.

Maisha: How old were you when you started with the Klan?

Tom: Seventeen.

Maisha: Only seventeen?

Tom: Yeah. And I began to read the stuff they gave me, go to their meetings. A lot of it was just pure hogwash, but when you're a teenager and you haven't had a chance to learn and develop critical-thinking skills—at least, I didn't when I was in school—then you're kind of ripe for these racist ideas.

The Ku Klux Klan didn't disappear when legal segregation ended. Here, hooded Klansmen demonstrate not in the Deep South but in Maryland, in 1982.

Maisha: Okay. If you believed all this, why did you leave the KKK?

Tom: We were putting a bomb at the home of a Jewish civil rights advocate in Meridian, Mississippi—myself and a young woman who was a schoolteacher—and the FBI found out. There was a big gun battle, and she was killed almost instantly. I was shot four times, and when I got to the hospital they said if I lived forty-five minutes, it would be a miracle.

Maisha: And that's when you left the Klan?

Tom: Not then. I escaped from prison, and was put back in, and began reading the Bible, the New Testament, and I came to realize that what I'd been doing was really evil. And that's when I got down on my knees and asked Jesus Christ to come into my life. Something changed inside. I became different. I've been different ever since. Once I realized God calls us to love people and there's no difference—I mean, the wrappers are different colors, but the people are the same.

Maisha: Did you tell people in the Klan they were wrong?

Tom: I wrote letters telling them what a terrible mistake we'd all been making. As you can imagine, they weren't too pleased. They hate blacks, they hate Jews, but they hate somebody like me much worse. In prison they got another inmate to try to kill me, which didn't work, obviously, or I wouldn't be sitting here.

Maisha: What message would you like to send to people now?

Tom: I think we're in a time where there's a growing anger and frustration among the races. The most important thing I could say is that it's possible for people to come together through the power of Jesus Christ. It worked for me, and nobody was more filled with hatred than I was, but I have lots of black and Jewish friends. We need this kind of modeling, see? A picture's worth a thousand words. You need to show people a relationship where black and white, or Hispanic, or Asian, have a real love and commitment toward each other.

Maisha: Your story's amazing.

Tom: It's just an example of the fact that nothing's impossible for God. You know, God spared my life, and I try to do as much good as I can while I'm here. It's very simple for me.

Christina Donovan with Demetrius Jordan and Maryam Brookins

Demetrius: I'm Demetrius Jordan. I'm twenty-three years old, and I just graduated from Morehouse College in Atlanta, Georgia.

Maryam: My name is Maryam Brookins, and I'm a senior at Georgetown University in Washington, D.C.

Christina: And I'm Christina Donovan, and I'm in the seventh grade. I'd like to know, Do you think discrimination has gotten better or worse since the 1960s?

Demetrius: In some ways it's gotten worse, in the sense that people are more creative at it. You can tie things up in the legal system.

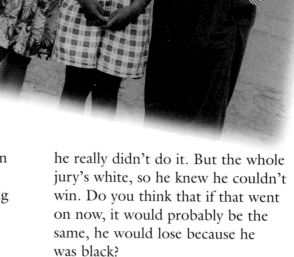

Maryam: That's right. Legally, African Americans have the law on their side, but that doesn't always mean it's going to work out for them.

Christina: We're reading a book now called *To Kill a Mockingbird,* and in it they say this black man, Tom Robinson, did something wrong, but he really didn't do it. But the whole jury's white, so he knew he couldn't win. Do you think that if that went on now, it would probably be the same, he would lose because he was black?

Maryam: Not always; things have changed—but isn't that similar to what happened with Rodney King? White policemen were seen beating him on videotape, yet an all-white jury found them innocent. It's sort of the opposite of what happens to Tom Robinson— this time it's white men found innocent of hurting a black man, but it's the same idea.

Christina: Well, what kinds of things do you think us kids can do about discrimination?

Maryam: I think the most important thing is to educate yourself about African American history and how

African Americans have been discriminated against in the past, and how that discrimination has evolved into something different today. And then, from there, to educate others.

Demetrius: I think about how our generation and your generation take for granted the civil rights movement. Just look at the difference between the number of people at the March on Washington in 1963—a quarter of a million—and the tens of thousands at the anniversary march in 1993.

Christina: Oh, yeah, the march on the

August 28, 1993: The thirtieth anniversary March on Washington.
Thirty years after Dr. King's famous "I Have a Dream" speech,
slogans like "Racism—Just Undo It" express the spirit of the day.

The Movement Shifts: The Struggle to End Poverty and Discrimination **119**

thirtieth anniversary of the big March on Washington. I was there with my mom and a bunch of other kids.

Demetrius: Great! It was good to see such a diverse group of people. There were a lot of white Americans and other groups like Hispanic and Native Americans, but there should have been more people, especially our age, making a difference, trying to meet the leaders.

Christina: Did you hear somebody say something at the 1993 march that you thought was so fantastic, everybody needs to hear it?

Maryam: I liked the way a lot of the speakers reemphasized the notion of having black pride and not forgetting about where you come from. If you have a chance to progress, to become rich or move out of whatever neighborhood, always pass your knowledge on to help others.

Demetrius: I like to hear African American leaders get up and say we shouldn't let the government, or anyone else, decide what our goals are, or our dreams, or how much we can achieve. No one can take away your determination unless you allow them to. And sometimes you do feel that you have to be twice as good as your white counterpart, but to me that's okay. I mean, why not? It's great to be good.

Christina: Right. Thank you both for this interview.

Rebecca and Carlos Lemos with Beatriz Otero and Arturo Flores

Rebecca: I'm Rebecca Lemos, and I'm with my brother, Carlos. We're interviewing our mother, BB Otero, and Carlos's teacher, Arturo Flores. Where were you both born and where did you grow up?

Beatriz: I am from La Paz, Bolivia, and I came to the United States when I was ten years old. I grew up in Washington, D.C.

Arturo: I was born in a barrio in El Paso, Texas. I grew up in California.

Carlos: What's a barrio?

Arturo: It's the Latino neighborhood of a city.

Rebecca: Okay. Even though you aren't

African Americans, did you ever feel discrimination?

Beatriz: When I came to Washington in the early 1960s, there weren't many Latinos. The fact that I was Spanish, that I spoke differently, that I had an accent, came up. I got into fights in school because I was called a spic.

Rebecca: What's a spic?

Beatriz: It's a word that puts down Spanish-speaking people. It made me angry to be called that.

Carlos: Mr. Flores, can you tell us about any times you were discriminated against?

Arturo: Yes. When I was graduating from high school, all my friends were talking about SATs and ACTs. You know what they are, right?

Beatriz Otero (right) joins then mayor Sharon Pratt Kelly of Washington, D.C., at a 1993 press conference of the Latino Task Force.

Carlos: No.

Arturo: Well, you will soon enough. Those are the tests you have to take if you want to go to college. I didn't know what they were either, so I asked my counselor. I had always been one of the best students and I thought he liked me. And Mr. Anderson said to me, "Well, Arthur—"

Carlos: Arthur? I thought your first name was—

Arturo: Arturo. It is. Back then they changed my name from Arturo to Arthur. "Arthur," he said, "you shouldn't worry about going to college. Thoughts like that will only break your heart because you won't make it."

Carlos: Even though you were one of the best students?

Arturo: Yes. But luckily, I didn't listen to him.

Beatriz: You know, there are Latinos in all parts of the United States who have this kind of experience.

Rebecca: Is that why you got involved with civil rights?

Beatriz: Having grown up in the 1960s, I think I always felt close to the civil rights movement, even when I was too young to participate. As I got older, it became a much wider movement, of women, of immigrants who do not have their fair share in this country. I've worked ever since high school to make sure Latinos have a good education, decent housing, the things we all need.

Rebecca: If there's one thing you could tell anyone out there, what would you tell them about civil rights?

Beatriz: That it's not an issue of twenty or thirty years ago—it's an issue of the present and will be an issue of the future. We are all valuable individuals, no matter where we come from, and we all have rights and responsibilities within this society. Civil rights today is an issue of human beings, and we must all be out there fighting for them.

Rebecca: Thank you, BB Otero.

Carlos: And thanks, you know, *muchas gracias,* Mr. Flores.

Elizabeth Wilkins with Roger Wilkins

Elizabeth: Hello. This is Elizabeth Wilkins reporting from home. Today I am interviewing my father. Let's begin. Did you take part in the civil rights movement?

Roger: Yes, I did a lot of marching in demonstrations— for example, the famous March on Washington where your great-uncle Roy Wilkins, who was then the leader of the NAACP, spoke. And I also participated as the director of an agency in the Department of Justice which did civil rights.

Elizabeth: Why did you participate?

Roger: Because I am an American who believes in the promise of the Constitution and the Declaration of Independence, and I am a black American who was deprived of my full rights as a citizen and whose ancestors were enslaved, and I wanted to help change the country. When black and white people live together in equality and freedom, it makes it a better country not just for black people, but for all people.

Elizabeth: Do you have any advice for kids now and in the future?

Roger: I think that decency and justice have to be worked for and fought for all the time. It's important for Americans to understand that the political rights we're granted under the Constitution are meant to be used. You have to vote, get involved in making your neighborhood a better place, support education, fair housing, and good medical care, maybe even run for office. If you think a law is unfair, write to your congressman, call the White House.

Elizabeth: You can do that?

Roger: You can do that. Someone will let the President know what you support. Sign petitions, march in demonstrations. People can change this country. When your uncle Roy and the NAACP fought segregation, a lot of people doubted it would ever change.

Elizabeth: But it did.

Roger: That's right, it did. And we still have the power to change for the better. It's not only an obligation, but the glory of being a free citizen under our Constitution.

Elizabeth: Thank you very much. This is Elizabeth Wilkins, signing off.

Important Events of the Civil Rights Movement

1954

May 17—Supreme Court rules in *Brown v. Board of Education* that segregated schools are illegal.

1955

December 1—Rosa Parks is arrested in Montgomery, Alabama, for not giving up her bus seat to a white person.

December 5—Montgomery bus boycott begins; it lasts until December 21, 1956.

1956

November 13—Supreme Court rules that segregation of Montgomery buses is illegal.

1957

January 10–11—Southern Christian Leadership Conference (SCLC) is founded with Martin Luther King, Jr., as president.

September—In Little Rock, Arkansas, National Guard and angry mobs prevent nine African American students from integrating white Central High School.

September 23—"Little Rock Nine" enter Central High for the first time. Two days later, on September 25, they receive protection from federal troops ordered in by President Dwight D. Eisenhower.

1960

February 1—In Greensboro, North Carolina, African American students "sit in" at a white lunch counter. Lunch counter sit-ins spread throughout the South.

April 15–17—Student Nonviolent Coordinating Committee (SNCC) is founded by students from nine states.

December 5—Supreme Court bans segregation in bus terminals.

1961

May–September—Congress of Racial Equality (CORE) "Freedom Riders" challenge segregation on interstate buses and in bus terminals; SNCC riders join them.

November—Albany Movement begins. Members of SNCC, NAACP, and Martin Luther King, Jr., work to end segregation in Albany, Georgia. The campaign ends unsuccessfully in August 1962.

1962

April 1—SNCC, SCLC, CORE, and NAACP form the Council of Federated Organizatons (COFO) to begin a united voter registration drive. Their first major project, "The Freedom Vote," begins in the fall of 1963.

September—Federal troops are needed to halt riots when African American James Meredith enters all-white University of Mississippi.

1963

April–May—Campaign for civil rights in Birmingham, Alabama, is led by Martin Luther King, Jr.

June 11—Alabama governor George Wallace stands in school doorway to stop integration of the University of Alabama.

June 12—Medgar Evers, leader of the Mississippi NAACP, is murdered.

August 28—March on Washington draws more than 250,000 people.

September 15—Four young African American girls are killed in bombing of Sixteenth Street Baptist Church in Birmingham, Alabama.

1964

January 23—Twenty-fourth Amendment to the Constitution outlaws poll tax in federal elections.

March—Malcolm X forms the Organization of Afro-American Unity after leaving the Nation of Islam.

June–August—"Freedom Summer": 1,000 young volunteers work to register voters in Mississippi.

June 21—Ku Klux Klan murders civil rights workers Michael Schwerner, James Chaney, and Andrew Goodman in Mississippi.

July 2—President Lyndon B. Johnson signs the Civil Rights Act into law.

1965

January–March—Voting rights campaign takes place in Selma, Alabama.

February 21—Malcolm X is assassinated in New York City.

August 6—President Lyndon B. Johnson signs Voting Rights Act into law.

August 11–16—African Americans riot in Watts, Los Angeles.

1966

June 16—Stokely Carmichael publicly uses term "Black Power," which signals a new direction for the movement.

October—Huey P. Newton and Bobby Seale start the Black Panther Party for Self-Defense in Oakland, California.

1967

October 2—Thurgood Marshall is sworn in as the first African American Supreme Court justice.

1968

April 4—Martin Luther King, Jr., is assassinated in Memphis, Tennessee.

For Further Study

Books

Darby, Jean. *Martin Luther King, Jr.* Minneapolis: Lerner Publications, 1990.

Duncan, Alice Faye. *The National Civil Rights Museum Celebrates Everyday People.* Mahwah, N.J.: Bridgewater Books, 1995.

Hampton, Henry, and Steve Fayer. *Voices of Freedom: An Oral History of the Civil Rights Movement from the 1950s Through the 1980s.* New York: Bantam Books, 1990.

Harris, Jacqueline. *History and Achievement of the NAACP.* New York: Franklin Watts, 1992.

Haskins, Jim. *Freedom Rides.* New York: Hyperion, 1995.

Haskins, Jim. *The March on Washington.* New York: HarperCollins, 1993.

Hughes, Langston, et al. *A Pictorial History of Black Americans.* New York: Crown, 1983.

King, Coretta Scott, ed. *The Words of Martin Luther King, Jr.* New York: Newmarket Press, 1983.

Levine, Ellen, ed. *Freedom's Children: Young Civil Rights Activists Tell Their Own Stories.* New York: Putnam, 1993.

McKissack, Patricia, and Fredrick McKissack. *The Civil Rights Movement in America from 1865 to the Present.* Chicago: Children's Press, 1987.

Myers, Walter Dean. *Malcolm X: By Any Means Necessary.* New York: Scholastic, 1993.

Myers, Walter Dean. *Now Is Your Time! The African-American Struggle for Freedom.* New York: HarperCollins, 1992.

Parks, Rosa, with Jim Haskins. *Rosa Parks: My Story.* New York: Dial Books, 1992.

Powledge, Fred. *We Shall Overcome: Heroes of the Civil Rights Movement.* New York: Scribners, 1993.

Ringgold, Faith. *My Dream of Martin Luther King.* New York: Crown, 1995.

Rochelle, Belinda. *Witnesses to Freedom: Young People Who Fought for Civil Rights.* New York: Lodestar, 1993.

Rowland, Della. *Martin Luther King, Jr.: The Dream of Peaceful Revolution.* Englewood Cliffs, N.J.: Silver Burdett Press, 1990.

Time-Life Books. *Perseverance.* African American Voices of Triumph series. Alexandria, Va., 1993.

Series

These two series on civil rights include biographies of prominent civil rights leaders:

Gateway Civil Rights by the Millbrook Press, Brookfield, Conn. Includes: John Brown, Stokely Carmichael, Frederick Douglass, W. E. B. Du Bois, Fannie Lou Hamer, Jesse Jackson, Martin Luther King, Jr., Abraham Lincoln, Malcolm X, Thurgood Marshall, Rosa Parks, A. Philip Randolph, Jackie Robinson, Sojourner Truth, Harriet Tubman, and Nat Turner.

History of the Civil Rights Movement by Silver Burdett Press, Englewood Cliffs, N.J. Includes: Ella Baker, Stokely Carmichael, Fannie Lou Hamer, Jesse Jackson, Martin Luther King, Jr., Malcolm X, Thurgood Marshall, Rosa Parks, and A. Philip Randolph.

Videos

The American Experience: Freedom on My Mind, a documentary about the dedicated students and sharecroppers who went to help organize voter registration in Mississippi during the summer of 1964. Produced and directed by Connie Field and Marilyn Mumford. Aired on PBS in 1995.

The American Experience: Malcolm X: Make It Plain, a documentary about the life of Malcolm X. Produced by Orlando Bagwell, Blackside, Inc. Available from PBS Video (800) 424-7963.

Eyes on the Prize I, a six-part PBS television series about the civil rights movement, focusing on the nonviolent fight to end legalized segregation. By Henry Hampton. First aired on PBS in 1986. Available from PBS Video (800) 424-7963.

Eyes on the Prize II, an eight-part sequel to Part 1 that aired on PBS in 1989 about the black nationalist movements during the civil rights era. By Henry Hampton, Blackside, Inc. Available from PBS Video (800) 424-7963.

Sources

Books

Branch, Taylor. *Parting the Waters: America in the King Years, 1954–63.* New York: Simon & Schuster, 1988.

Breitman, George, ed. *Malcolm X Speaks: Selected Speeches and Statements.* New York: Grove Press, 1966.

Carson, Clayborne. *In Struggle: SNCC and the Black Awakening of the 1960s.* Cambridge, Mass.: Harvard University Press, 1981.

Carson, Clayborne, et al., eds. *The Eyes on the Prize Civil Rights Reader: Documents, Speeches and Firsthand Accounts from the Black Freedom Struggle, 1954–1990.* New York: Penguin Books, 1991.

Egerton, John. *Speak Now Against the Day: The Generation Before the Civil Rights Movement in the South.* New York: Knopf, 1994.

Fager, Charles E. *Selma, 1965: The March That Changed the South.* Boston: Beacon Press, 1974.

Garrow, David. *Bearing the Cross: Martin Luther King, Jr., and the Southern Christian Leadership Conference.* New York: Morrow, 1986.

Ianniello, Lynne, ed. *Milestones Along the March: Twelve Historic Civil Rights Documents from World War II to Selma.* New York: Praeger, 1965.

Lyon, Danny. *Memories of the Southern Civil Rights Movement.* Chapel Hill, N.C.: University of North Carolina Press, 1992.

Malcolm X. *The Autobiography of Malcolm X, As Told to Alex Haley.* New York: Grove Press, 1964.

Perry, Bruce, ed. *Malcolm X: The Last Speeches.* New York: Pathfinder, 1989.

Seale, Bobby. *Seize the Time: The Story of the Black Panther Party and Huey P. Newton.* New York: Random House, 1970; Baltimore: Black Classic Press, 1991.

Sitkoff, Harvard. *The Struggle for Black Equality, 1954–1992.* New York: Hill and Wang, 1993.

Ture, Kwame (Stokely Carmichael), and Charles Hamilton. *Black Power: The Politics of Liberation*. New York: Random House, 1967.

Washington, James M., ed. *A Testament of Hope: The Essential Writings and Speeches of Martin Luther King, Jr.* San Francisco: Harper & Row, 1986.

Weisbrot, Robert. *Freedom-Bound: A History of America's Civil Rights Movement*. New York: Norton, 1990.

White, John. *Black Leadership in America, 1895–1968*. New York: Longman, 1985.

Yette, Frederick Walton, and Samuel F. Washington Yette. *Two Marches, 1963 & 1983: The Third American Revolution*. Silver Spring, Md.: Cottage Books, 1984.

Video
Hampton, Henry. *Eyes on the Prize I*, a six-part PBS television series on the civil rights movement from 1954 to 1965. First aired on PBS in 1986. Available from PBS Video (800) 424-7963.

Recordings
Voices of the Civil Rights Movement: Black American Freedom Songs, 1960–1966. (Two-record collection). Washington, D.C.: Smithsonian Institution Program in Black American Culture, 1980.

Acknowledgments

Oh, Freedom! began in 1989 at St. Anthony's Grade School in Washington, D.C. I had started to teach my fourth graders about the civil rights movement and was surprised to find that they had only minimal knowledge of the facts and little or no sense of how the movement had touched the lives of their families, neighbors, and friends.

In response, I told them that we'd be writing our own personal history of the civil rights movement. After covering the basics of the movement, I taught them simple interview techniques. They practiced on each other. Then for homework they went out into their neighborhoods, armed with tape recorders and questions they had written, to find history.

The reaction to the assignment was tremendous. Adults who were interviewed were thrilled that children were interested in hearing about their experiences, and the students were surprised and proud to learn of the many personal connections their own families and friends had to historic events.

Encouraged by the outpouring of enthusiasm, I spoke to Linda, the mother of one of my students, about a collaborative effort to expand the project into a book. Seven years later, after working with over 500 children and collecting over 2,000 pages of stories, the book is finally done. We hope the intergenerational dialogue will continue.

We would like to give special thanks to the following people who made this book possible: Barbara Bullock, who inspired the original oral history project; the principals, teachers, and librarians who welcomed us into their schools and classrooms: Sister Francene Van Eck, John Devereaux, Lucinda Jasper, Sharon Jones, Jane Sampugnaro, Rita Zito, Alvira Travis, Melissa Fulcher Hinkson, Charles Epps, Shirley Collins, Patricia Greer, Pamela Korbel, Julie Simon, Robert Williams, Sandra Dennin, Mary Downey, and Kathleen O'Neill; Jim Huffman of the Schomburg Center for Research in Black Culture for special help with photographs; Regina Kahney and Jill Davis for their tireless efforts at developing this book; Washington Area Lawyers for the Arts; Lisa Banim, Olivia King Canter, Paul Coates, James Early, Leslie Jones, Bob Osborne, Catherine Osborne, Nick Osborne, Marlon Riggs, Karen Spellman, Elaine Steele, Julee Thompson, Bob Vivona, Nicholas Vivona, and Samuel Yette for their suggestions, support, aid at a moment's notice, and faith in this project. We could not have done this alone and apologize to anyone we might have overlooked.

We would also like to thank all those who participated in the oral history project but did not appear in the book, including Stuart Adams, Alan Cheuse, Annie Dickerson, Lucius Outlaw, Deborah Smith, Lou Stovall, William Taylor, Tom Waldron, and Jim Wells; and the students:

Luca Adelfio	Sean Byrd	Jessica DeVille
Al-Nisaa Ahmad	Genise Chambers	Andre Diggs
Idara Akpan	Nicholas Chanock	Margaret Doles
Robert Alves	Sonya Cheuse	Latrice Earl
Gene Arlook	Marqus Clark	JaBen Early
Kimberly Arnold	Tara Coles	Malinda Farmer
Adeline Barillas	Lawrence Coley	Krystal Ferguson
Thomas Bolden	Lovon Colter	Julius Ford
Ayana Briscoe	April Conway	Thomas Frampton
Janine Brunson	Jeena Daramola	Nick Friedman
James Byrd	Benjamin Davison	Sharmane Grady

Ashley Greenfield
Lei-Loni Greenhow
Jacob Grossman
Markus Ham
Sara Harlow
Chiquita Harmon
Alesha Hicks
James Hoban
Bernard Holt
Yale Howard
Brandon Huges
Njena Jarvis
Amir Jenkins
Dorothy Jones
Kerron Kalloo
Michelle Katzow
Roy Kelly
Erika Kendrick
Zachary Knight
Brian Lewis
Ebony Long
Cheryl Lucas
Danielle Mack
Marcus Mack

Quinn Mahoney
John Mathews
Dawn Medley
Tania Mena
Delia Meneely-Sepulvado
Chalmus Miles
Nyah Molineaux
Roberto Montesinos
Luke Motsuk
Anthony Njohu
Jeremy Oldfield
Raynita Orange
Nicole Otey
Kofi Outlaw
Sharron Patterson
Christen Pone
Colleen Powell
Mary Powell
Reginald Rich
Minke Richardson
Rosenda Rosas
Crystal Rucker
Joshua Russell
Lashawnda Rust
Brandon Scott

Tomasha Sears
Susie Senerchia
Leo Sheridan
Aaron Smith
Amina Smith
Samar Smith
Thomas Spencer
Douglas Stancil
Danielle Stassien
Adam Suddoo
Dev Talvadkar
Corleon Taylor
Eleanor Terry
Lindsay Tomar
Eua Umoh
Koran Washington
Marquette Washington
Fema Watson
William Wilson
Joanna Wood
Stephen Wood
Tiffany Worsley
Aundrea Wright
Taiysha Wright

—Casey King

Index

Photographic Acknowledgments

AP/Wide World Photos: pages 35, 40–41, 44, 82-83, 89.

The Birmingham News. Copyright © 1997 by *The Birmingham News*. All rights reserved. Reprinted by permission: pages 42–43.

Black Star/Charles Moore: page 66.

Joe Brooks: pages 12, 14, 16, 18, 20, 22, 24, 25, 28, 50, 53, 56, 59, 62, 65, 68, 70, 73, 76, 79, 94, 97, 103, 106, 109, 112, 115, 118, 121, 124.

Brown Brothers: page 5.

Paul Coates: page 104.

Culver Pictures: page 4.

Charles Epps: page 13.

Ruth Jackson: page 54.

Casey King: pages 99, 119.

Library of Congress: pages 9, 15.

Library of Congress, Prints & Photographs Division, *U.S. News & World Report* Magazine Collection: pages 71 [LC-U9-10358], 113 [LC-U9-18953, frame 25].

Magnum Photos, Inc.: pages 46–47 (Danny Lyon), 60 and 77 (Danny Lyon) from the book *Memories of the Southern Civil Rights Movement*, 74 (Danny Lyon), 84–85 (Eve Arnold).

Ethel Minor: page 96.

Phay Collection, University of Mississippi Special Collections: pages 30–31.

El Pregonero; photo by Michael Alexander: pages 92, 122.

Malaya Rucker: page 27.

Schomburg Center for Research in Black Culture, Photographs and Prints Division, The New York Public Library, Astor, Lenox, and Tilden Foundations: pages 3, 7, 8, 13, 17, 23, 57, 86.

Karen Spellman: pages 58.

UPI/Bettmann: pages 38–39, 81, 105.

UPI/Corbis-Bettmann: pages 48–49, 72, 87, 90–91, 101.

The Washington Post. Copyright © *The Washington Post*, reprinted by permission of the D.C. Public Library: pages 10–11, 19, 26, 32–33, 51, 63, 69, 75, 95, 107, 111.

Dan Weiner, courtesy of Sandra Weiner: pages 36–37.

Samuel F. Yette Copyright © 1982 by Samuel F. Yette. All rights reserved. Reprinted by permission: page 116.